LOST LUGGAG
OUTRAGEOUS
YOU DON'T H
TAKE IT ANY

Isn't it time that your luggage arrives when you
do? That you leave and arrive on schedule?
That your seats are comfortable? That you
don't lose your money when you cancel your
flight? And that you find low fares without
unreasonable restrictions?

READY FOR TAKE-OFF is the first serious,
up-to-date guide that shows how you can get
where you are going by air without the common
frustrations and safety risks so many passengers
tolerate. Here is coveted insider information
designed to save you money, calm your fears,
and get you to your destination on time and
with the least number of problems.

You may already be an experienced traveler.
Now become a smart one.

READY FOR TAKE-OFF

The Complete Passenger's Guide to Safer,
Smarter Air Travel

READY FOR TAKE-OFF

The Complete Passenger's Guide to Safer, Smarter Air Travel

Marie Hodge and Jeff Blyskal

A SIGNET BOOK

SIGNET
Published by the Penguin Group
Penguin Books USA Inc., 375 Hudson Street,
New York, New York 10014, U.S.A.
Penguin Books Ltd, 27 Wrights Lane,
London W8 5TZ, England
Penguin Books Australia Ltd, Ringwood,
Victoria, Australia
Penguin Books Canada Ltd, 2801 John Street,
Markham, Ontario, Canada L3R 1B4
Penguin Books (N.Z.) Ltd, 182-190 Wairau Road,
Auckland 10, New Zealand

Penguin Books Ltd, Registered Offices:
Harmondsworth, Middlesex, England

First published by Signet, an imprint of New American Library,
a division of Penguin Books USA Inc.

First Printing, April, 1991
10 9 8 7 6 5 4 3 2 1

Portions of this book first appeared in *New York* magazine as
"Your Airline Survival Guide."

 REGISTERED TRADEMARK—MARCA REGISTRADA

Printed in the United States of America

To Paul and Dorothy

Contents

CHAPTER 1

Consumer Power Takes to the Air

The purpose of this book is to help you get the best service you're paying for from U.S. and foreign air carriers. The practical advice from *Ready for Take-off* will improve your chances of getting the lowest fares, avoiding major hassles, finding top-drawer cabin service, and arriving at your destination on time—and in one piece.

But there's more to smooth air travel than just getting your money's worth—unpleasant travel experiences can cause consequent damages. If you're a business traveler, you know how poor-quality air travel can undercut your out-of-town business dealings: cramped, uncomfortable seating can leave you ill-prepared for meetings, a frustrating run-in with a ticket clerk can burn up energy needed at the negotiating table, and late or canceled flights can cost you clients.

Vacation travelers also suffer losses from poor-quality airline service. A fatiguing, stress-filled airline trip reduces the value of your entire vacation. Other air travel problems, like expensive changes in flight plans, and delays, can ruin your vacation budget. *Ready for Take-off* will help preserve the value of the business or pleasure you're flying to.

The Frustration of Air Travel

Unfortunately, the airline passenger of the nineties needs protection from an onslaught of foulups and headaches created by airlines and the government agencies that regulate them. If you have flown within the past 12 months, you know the present state of air travel is discomforting, dismal, and dangerous. For example:

• In Sarasota, FL, Kenneth Christman says he and a packed planeload of other passengers sat on a sweltering Continental Airlines DC-9 while the flight and ground crews spent 2 hours trying to figure out how to fold up the plane's retractable stairs.

• In Washington's Dulles International Airport, Reinhard Stoye was delayed 13 hours and had to buy a night's hotel stay when his connecting flight from Germany to Raleigh/Durham, NC, on Presidential Airlines was canceled. Next morning there was another irritating surprise: the 8:55 A.M. flight was late and did not depart until 9:40 A.M.

• In New York, USAir Captain Michael W. Martin and First Officer Constantine Kleissas *simply disappeared* for 36 hours after they aborted takeoff and crashed their Boeing 737-400 with 63 passengers and crew on board into Riker's

Island Channel near LaGuardia Airport. The crash of flight 5050 killed two passengers and injured 45 others.

• In Minneapolis/St. Paul, Terry Hagelthorn says she waited at the baggage carousel for luggage containing her clothes and important business papers. She didn't get them; Continental Airlines had sent the bags to Cleveland. Next day, Hagelthorn missed her morning meetings waiting for her luggage to arrive—they didn't show up until 9 P.M. On the return to Newark, Hagelthorn recalls Continental lost the bags again. She says the airline delivered the bags the next night, leaving them unprotected on Hagelthorn's front porch in Weehawken, NJ.

• At Washington's National Airport another traveler almost missed her Northwest Airlines flight to San Francisco because, she remembers, she was stuck for 2 hours in Northwest's ticket, baggage-check, and boarding-gate lines. Bad weather forced the plane to land in Duluth, and additional delays were caused by late flight crews and the plane's running out of fuel. She finally arrived in "the City by the Bay" at 1:30 A.M. after 12 exhausting hours of air travel.

• In Fargo, ND, an intoxicated Northwest Airlines captain and cockpit crew took off in a Boeing 727 with 91 passengers on board and flew to Minneapolis. The crew—which had allegedly been out drinking and had stopped mere hours before their flight's 6:30 A.M. scheduled departure —was apprehended in a citizen's arrest by Douglas Solseth, an FAA inspector in Minneapolis.

In August 1990, a federal jury in Minneapolis found the pilot, copilot, and flight engineer guilty of flying an airliner while under the influence of alcohol. All three are appealing the verdict.

According to an investigation by *The Minneapolis Star Tribune,* at least 41 pilots of passenger aircraft lost their Minnesota driver's licenses in the last seven years because of drunken driving or lesser alcohol-related motor vehicle offenses. To get that information, the newspaper did what the FAA could have done; cross-matching an FAA listing of Minnesota residents who hold an air transport license with state and court records showing alcohol-related driving violations between 1983 and 1990.

In December 1988, 259 passengers and crew on Pan Am flight 103 from Frankfurt to New York via London were blown out of the sky over Lockerbie, Scotland, by a terrorist's bomb.

Incredibly, even after the bombing, FAA inspectors said that Pan Am repeatedly violated antiterrorist security regulations and failed to hand-search checked, noncarry-on luggage, the kind of baggage most likely to contain a bomb. Pan Am's alleged high-risk behavior continued for eight months *after* the tragedy. According to James Weidner, executive director of President Bush's special commission of inquiry into the bombing, in June 1989, one FAA inspector's report said that Pan Am security in Frankfurt was "totally unsatisfactory. Major violations in all areas. Posture considered unsafe. All passengers flying out of Frankfurt on Pan Am are at great risk."

Pan Am did not repair its Frankfurt security system until September 1989, when the FAA finally slapped the airline with a $630,000 fine for numerous violations of security rules in the boarding of flight 103.

Pan Am spokesman Jeff Kriendler says the airline disputes "every one of" the FAA charges, admits no wrongdoing, and has not paid the fine. "Pan Am security never compromised passenger safety," he says.

Close Relationship: Airlines and the Regulators

Unfortunately, you cannot depend upon federal overseers to take care of you. In the wake of the Airline Deregulation Act of 1978, they've abdicated responsibility for problems at every level, from the most mundane to the most serious. The present regulatory apparatus is so Kafkaesque, examples of illogical bureaucratic logic abound.

For instance, despite numerous congressional committee investigations and studies of airline practices detrimental to consumers, despite an increase in state-level actions against airlines, and despite surveys showing that most consumers think air travel has deteriorated, the U.S. Department of Transportation (USDOT) believes the flying public is satisfied with service. "I'm happy to report that consumers are pretty happy with air travel at the moment," says Hoyte Decker, the USDOT's assistant director of consumer affairs. "More than 453 million people flew last year; we got 12,403 complaints. That's a very insignificant number."

At the same time, the USDOT has fought tenaciously to protect *airlines* from consumers. Since 1988, the USDOT has actually waged pitched battle against the attorneys general of 32 states to protect airlines' attempts to mislead consumers with deceptive advertising practices. A 1988 General Accounting Office study concluded that consumers would benefit if the USDOT worked *with* the state attorneys rather than against them.

The same study found flaws in the USDOT's consumer protection activities. The USDOT is the clearinghouse for consumer airline complaints, but it does not systematically follow up on cases to ensure that complaints have been satisfactorily resolved. Sometimes, the department misses obvious cases of abuse warranting further investigation. In 1987, after the department received 28 complaints about one air travel agency not properly refunding money, the USDOT did nothing to pursue the company. In an independent action later that year, another government agency, the Federal Trade Commission, shut down the company and froze its assets for fraudulent activity.

In yet another bizarre twist of justice, when the USDOT did undertake a special investigation of consumer complaints about airline scheduling delays, the department negotiated a settlement with the airlines which set a new late-flight standard *below* the level that had prompted all the complaints. Thus, the USDOT investigation caused consumers to actually lose ground and won the airlines a better deal than they had before the trouble started.

The Federal Aviation Administration isn't doing the best job possible to protect passengers either. According to a recent audit by the General Accounting Office, the FAA has failed to perform thousands of required airplane and airline maintenance base inspections in recent years because of understaffing. One unnamed airline was not inspected for all of 1988, said the GAO. According to an article in *The New York Times*, "Crash investigators say lapses in these inspections have contributed to several recent fatal accidents."

Examples of FAA laxity are not hard to find. According to the National Transportation Safety Board, the FAA contributed to the death of 14 passengers in the 1988 crash of a Delta Air Lines Boeing 727 at Dallas/Ft. Worth Airport. In a shocking indictment one year later, the NTSB found that the FAA—which is supposed to protect the safety of air passengers—actually *contributed* to the accident by not adequately monitoring and cracking down on Delta after a series of incidents and accidents. "I believe that the FAA and Delta were *direct* causes of the accident," argued NTSB board member Jim Burnett at a public hearing discussing the accident.

Nor does the FAA rush to protect the public from aircraft flaws or outdated safety standards. "The FAA is extremely reluctant to take any meaningful action involving mechanical or design problems—even when they're known—until someone or a large number of people get killed," says Eugene Garges, Jr., a retired airline pilot. For example, the FAA's inaction has made fatalities out of passengers who might have survived some airline crashes. Reason: the agency's refusal to mandate a negligibly more expensive and significantly more crashworthy airline passenger seat. The FAA has known about the easily correctible problem for almost 30 years now. The stronger 16-G seats (which are discussed further in Chapter 3) are such an obvious asset, some major airlines are installing them even though the regulations don't require it.

In 1982, the FAA actually proposed a regulation that would have eliminated many existing safety standards for airlines. In place of strict rules and requirements, the FAA would have provided suggested guidelines for each airline to follow as it sees fit. A firestorm of opposition ultimately killed the idea.

Even in the high-priority war against terrorism, regulators remain flat-footed. According to a report by Paul Wilkinson, a professor at Scotland's University of St. Andrews and an expert on international terrorism, airlines, airports, and governments have done little to improve security since Pan Am flight 103 was destroyed by a bomb.

Indeed, the Bush commission investigating the Pan Am bombing concluded that the FAA's airline security program is "seriously flawed" and "needs major reform."

"Another Lockerbie could happen tomorrow," says Wilkinson.

Consumers Still Call the Shots

Clearly, today's airline passenger has to fend for himself. However, with a little know-how and the power to vote with the dollars in your pocket, you *can* take care of yourself.

But to take charge of the air chaos, you must banish any self-defeating images of the "consumer as victim." Only losers get taken, and today's smart air travel consumers are most definitely *not* losers—unless they choose to be. Airline deregulation has given consumers greater power to dictate terms to the airlines, both in individual situations and en masse, as we will see shortly.

Sure, passengers may get roughed up a bit. The airline business is still very much a dogfight right now, with big investors battling for control of big airlines. Northwest, Piedmont, Eastern, People Express—the list of friendly and fierce takeovers goes on and on. Big airlines are battling each other for big pieces of the market. Some big employee unions and managers have stood ready to destroy their airlines to get what they want in the rumble (witness Eastern Airlines' protracted labor/management war).

So no one can expect consumers to come out of this brawl without a bloody nose. And why should they? Consumers are big players too: they control the $54 billion a year in revenues that everyone is fighting over.

Consumers hold more cards than they realize. All the tough-talking chief executive officers, the airline marketing people, the unions, and the big money boys financing buyouts are in the game to serve the consumer, not the other way around. Sufficiently dissatisfied with an airline's quality of service, pricing, marketing practices, safety consciousness, or food, fickle consumers can always take their business to a competitor. That's not just textbook economic theory or pie-in-the-sky thinking about free markets, that's a rule of the game. Customers can exert real power by voting with their dollars.

Pan Am, once the standard in air travel, was brought to its knees because its service deteriorated terribly in the eighties. Mad-as-hell customers vowed they wouldn't take it sitting down anymore. Without professional organization or a sophisticated game plan for rebellion, customers used the immense power of their ultimate weapon: they simply took their business elsewhere.

Frank Lorenzo's Lesson

Pan Am is not the only airline that rough customer justice made into an example. When passengers stand up for themselves, airlines respond.

Take Continental, which has had a reputation for dreadful service since its mergers with People Express and Frontier Airlines in 1987. "Travel agents had been booking customers *away* from Continental," says Kevin Murphy, an airline stock analyst at Morgan Stanley & Co. In 1988, Continental was the most complained-about airline in the U.S. skies. From 1987 to 1989, Continental posted more than $500 million in losses, and nothing concentrates an airline's attention on its customers' needs like a half-billion dollars in red ink.

Frank Lorenzo, the Continental chairman at the time, who was considered tough-as-nails by industry watchers and worse than an SOB by labor, cowered in the face of this warning from consumers. The airline was forced to shape up, and it has been working hard to clean up its act. "Continental's service has gotten better," says Murphy. "Traffic is up and service is improving."

In 1989, Lorenzo slashed the complaint rate by 75 percent and Continental was number 7 in customer complaints. The customer spoke, and big bad Frank Lorenzo listened.

That's *your* key to good service. Airlines will jump through hoops for the customer. But consumers have to be tough enough to *make* them do it.

How to Be a Tough Customer

How do you make an airline jump for you? By doing your job as an educated consumer. If low fares are important to you, don't just take an airline ticket agent's word that you're paying the lowest fare. Do your homework and *find* the lowest fare. Chapter 4 will tell you how to do it.

Smart consumers are also aware of their options. Service quality is not the same on every airline, because the managers of each airline have different ideas about what the customer wants and varying opinions about what constitutes good service. Chapters 5 and 6 will help guide you through the airline options that give you consumer power through freedom of choice.

Today's sophisticated air travelers must also know their rights *and their responsibility* to persuade airline personnel to give them the service they deserve. Only 1 in 2,000 victims of mishandled baggage files a complaint with the USDOT; just 1 in 25,000 files a complaint when his plane is late or canceled. Chapter 7 shows how to complain effectively and—more important—*how to get action.*

Some things you can't control, especially accidents and acts of terrorism. Bad weather, faulty equipment, poor maintenance, an inexperienced pilot, or just plain fate may be at work to set up a date with destiny for you. But you *can* still take some safety precautions to reduce your chances of stepping onto a doomed flight. Chapters 2 and 3 spell out what you need to know to protect yourself from the airlines, the bombers, and the bureaucrats.

Learn the Gritty Details

Finally, the savvy air traveler has a practical, how-does-it-affect-me understanding of airline industry operations and such big-picture issues as deregulation, labor/management disputes, and air safety. Throughout, *Ready for Take-off* takes you inside the business of air travel and interprets how airline policies, behind-the-scenes practices and procedures, operating economies, and esoteric details have an impact on you, your wallet, your safety, and the quality of your flight. Only by seeing air travel from both sides—from the consumer's *and* the airline's vantage points—can you accurately weigh trade-offs and effectively assess whether you're getting your money's worth.

For instance, to compete on price, airlines must reduce their costs as much as possible. One way to do this is with an efficient hub-and-spoke route system: instead of flying directly from every airport to every airport, airlines gather up people at the end of a "spoke" and fly them to a centrally located hub. From there, the passengers fly down different spokes to their individual destinations. Highly efficient companies such as Federal Express move packages the same way.

What does this mean for you? There are pluses and minuses. More short-hop flights, more connecting flights, longer traveling time, and more crowded flights are some of the negatives. On the positive side, however, people living in smaller communities gain greater access to the airline network, and prices in general are kept down. The environment even benefits a little; pound-for-pound of pollution, airlines today are squeezing more productivity out of their jet exhaust.

You may be unhappy about not having an empty seat next to you on one of these efficiently packed flights. On average, today's planes fly 61 percent filled with passengers versus 54 percent full before deregulation, according to the Air Transport Association. Most people, however, are willing to put up with connecting flights and more crowded planes in exchange for as low an airfare as possible. The point is this: both passengers—the one who wants comfort and the one who wants a price bargain—can usually have their needs fulfilled, if they know what they're doing. This book will give you the information you need to know.

Look Behind the Myths

A clear understanding of airline operations will give you the sophistication necessary to separate myths—fostered by special interest groups—from unvarnished reality. That's important, because your time is valuable and you don't need to waste it chasing after phony bargains. Unfortunately, because of the stakes in this $54 billion-a-year business, plenty of groups stand ready to persuade or dissuade you—for *their* benefit.

For example, airlines and regulators perpetuate the myth that no section of a plane is safer than any other in a crash. That's just not true. We know, because *Ready for Take-off* has done the only publicly available research on the subject. As explained in Chapter 3, the hard data prove that on average, passengers seated in the front section of the plane tend to take the brunt of most crashes, whereas those in the rear third of the plane have the best chance of surviving. Of course, because every accident is different, there is no guarantee you'll survive a crash if seated in the rear section of the plane, but your chances of survival there are statistically greater.

The media are another interest group. They

promote the image of the "Consumer as victim," because bad news sells. Consequently, the press frequently overemphasizes the negative effects of deregulation. There can be no denying that deregulation was a tumultuous experience, and that customers did get buffeted by the winds of change. But overall, consumers have come out ahead under deregulation, because airlines have more freedom and flexibility to give customers what they want.

Before deregulation, generous minimum airfares were set by the government. Because all same-class fares on the same route were the same for every airline, no one could cut prices to lure customers away from the competition. So the airlines distinguished themselves from the competition with better service. United's "friendly skies" slogan aimed to grab customers who encountered unfriendly skies with other airlines.

But in the inflation-plagued seventies, customers began to demand airfares that were not artificially propped up by the government. Deregulation allowed price competition, and airlines gave customers what they wanted. No-frills People Express experienced boom growth with a low price strategy. Soon, other airlines were forced to compete on price—at the expense of service quality.

Members of Congress, the media, and customers have complained about today's high fares and wondered where the savings are. But if you factor out inflation, the savings are there. Although some fares on certain routes have gone through the roof, on average, inflation-adjusted airfares today are considerably lower than they were before deregulation. Rational consumer behavior also proves that flying is a bigger bargain today. Consumer demand for air travel has skyrocketed. The 454-million passenger boardings in 1989 were up 64 percent above the 277 million in 1978, the year the airlines were deregulated. Basic economic law says a demand shift like that is inspired by *lower* prices, not higher prices.

Unfortunately, this explosion has stretched the air travel system to the limits. "Flying has become so popular, it's now hard to run it efficiently," says Bruce Nobles, president of the Trump Shuttle. "Planes are full; airports are crowded; getting to the airport is difficult." According to a survey of fliers by *Consumer Reports* magazine, almost 50 percent said the quality of air travel under deregulation has deteriorated; just 20 percent said it has improved. With public attention focused on service problems, the emphasis for airlines has shifted back to service. That means airlines will have to figure out how much price and how much service to deliver, which, in turn, means greater variation from airline to airline and even from one route to another. Through it all, though, it is the consumer who is calling the shots, not the airlines.

Knowing the real story can help prepare you for the future. In the eighties and early nineties, European airlines have provided top-quality cabin service compared with that of U.S. airlines. Is that just another example of America's inability to compete? If you fly to Europe in 1995, should you, without hesitation, fly a European airline instead of a good U.S. carrier? The answer to both questions is no. European airlines have enjoyed an unfair advantage over their U.S. competitors— price-supported regulation by government treaties. Although U.S. airlines have been competing on price or on price *and* service, the Europeans have only had to compete on service. Is it any wonder they are so successful?

In 1992, however, the playing field is scheduled to be made more level. That's when European airlines are expected to be fully deregulated. Consequently, that will likely spark the same rough-and-tumble price *and* service competition U.S. airlines have had to deal with, although resistance to deregulation by some European governments and airlines may slow down and soften the negative effects. Nevertheless, juggling the two balls isn't easy, so expect increased turmoil in your European air travel in the coming years as the airlines become more market-oriented.

One emerging strategy is the linkup of U.S. and European carriers through partial interownership and partnership agreements. Delta and Swissair, Northwest and KLM, and Continental and SAS have all forged bonds aimed at having passengers fed to them by their partners. (Similar arrangements feed passengers back and forth between major airlines and small commuter airline partners.) For the companies, these agreements give the partners toeholds in each other's markets, improve efficiency, and create somewhat captive markets.

How does this impact you? For Delta's U.S. customers flying on to an international destination not served by Delta, the Delta/Swissair connection means passengers will likely be herded toward Swissair. That may be a perfect match, but complacent customers *may* miss a better deal or better service flying a nonpartner airline.

Another Euro problem on the horizon is air traffic control. The European air traffic system has gotten woefully congested, and by 1995 air gridlock over Europe will be "catastrophic," predicts a report by the International Air Transport Association, an airline trade group. That can only mean less than punctual service, more crowded planes, less pleasant summer travel, and perhaps rising airfares to cover the multibillion-dollar cost of alleviating air congestion.

Keeping up to date with airline issues like these and understanding the many and varied relationships affecting the industry will help keep you ahead of the airlines, and ahead of the game. *Ready for Take-off* provides the information you need to get started.

CHAPTER 2

Personal Air Safety—Part I

What You Can Do *Now* to Protect Yourself from
Air Crashes, Unsafe Airlines, and Terrorists
Before You Book Reservations

You are flying a Boeing 727-200 with 107 passengers on board. Approximately 30 minutes prior to landing, there is a strange bump. The plane jostles you, then noticeably loses altitude. There are changes in the muffled, whining background noise of the engines, your ears pop, the plane pitches to the left. You and the other passengers, sensing danger, grow concerned.

Experienced flyers know that most in-flight noises and aircraft movements are no cause for alarm. In this case, however, the combination of sounds and motion is a warning: your plane is about to crash. In a moment, the flight attendants will confirm that. Already, concerned looks on their faces and a sudden flurry of activity indicate an emergency.

The captain, who has partial control of his jet, plans to do his best to land as normally as possible by sidling up to the ground, wheels down—making this what accident investigators and safety experts will call a survivable crash. Approximately

98 percent of U.S. scheduled airline accidents involving larger aircraft over the last 20 years were totally or partially survivable, so your chances of getting out of an accident alive are actually excellent.

But who survives and who dies? The outcome is based partly on fate and partly on each passenger's survival skill.

Here, based on eyewitness accounts and investigative data from scores of accidents involving both survivors and fatalities since 1970, is a compilation of what you would most likely experience in a survivable air crash. The accident data base involves all types of passenger aircraft, weather conditions, causes, and impact scenarios. Some details are unlikely but nevertheless *possible* and worth being prepared for. Throughout, watch for the fatal mistakes you must avoid.

Warning

Panic and pandemonium do not sweep through the cabin, the way it happens in a Hollywood movie. Passengers have none of the facts others will read about in tomorrow's newspapers: they don't know how it will all turn out, so they are contemplative, quiet, waiting for whatever information or instructions they can get.

"Ladies and gentlemen, the captain has just told us to prepare for an emergency landing. Please be seated immediately in the nearest seat and fasten your seat belt. Secure all carry-on items under your seat, return tray tables to their closed position, and move seat backs upright."

Meanwhile, your body begins readying its own crisis response mechanisms. Your endocrine system reflexively starts dumping adrenaline into your bloodstream. Heart rate and breathing begin to quicken. Your fingers have gained a tighter grip on the armrest as all your body's muscles tense. Blood vessels have constricted and your stomach has stopped digesting the in-flight meal. Nerve receptors and your senses of touch, sight, and sound have become more sensitive and give you a heightened feeling of awareness.

The warning, which many passengers and flight crews never get, may give you 30 minutes to prepare—or 30 seconds.

Impact

No matter how much advance notice you are lucky to have, impact comes much sooner than expected. Again, this is not a movie with an hour for you to learn how Shelley Winters or George Kennedy will bear up under the strain or how Charlton Heston will pilot the plane to a safe, though spark-filled landing. Reality departs from carefully scripted plots.

Every impact is different. Some passengers report a relatively mild, almost smooth crash experience, whereas others live through violent motions and rapid deceleration. The crash forces you experience depend on how close to parallel (or, at the worst extreme, perpendicular) the plane is when it comes in contact with the ground. It also depends on the levelness of the terrain and what objects and structures the plane crashes into.

These unpredictable factors determine how much impact energy is transmitted to the aircraft and, from there, to your body.

There is a loud "bang!" then a rushing sound. Another bang, scraping, and unidentified noise. None of it makes sense.

On impact you will probably not be totally aware of what's happening to your body. As the plane impacts and skids to a stop, your upper torso may flail like a rag doll. The greatest G-forces—multiples of gravity—will likely be in a forward direction and on your pelvic and spinal areas as the seat belt holds you tight. Properly secured around the bones of your hips and pelvis, the belt is less likely to damage abdominal muscles and organs. You will, nevertheless, receive black-and-blue marks, cuts, or bruises from a seat belt that does its job in a rough impact.

Meanwhile, overhead storage compartments have sprung open, and carry-on items cascade out and toward the front of the plane. Entire overhead compartments themselves collapse and fall along with ceiling tiles. Broken plastic, metal, and hardware spray through the air and lacerate your arms. A 12-pound transportable personal computer flies out and forward, hitting the woman in seat 22C. Moving forward with the force of 8 G's, the computer slams into the woman's head as though it weighed 96 pounds, seriously injuring her. Other heavy objects fly through the cabin like cannonballs at a speed slightly less than the plane was traveling at before impact.

In the rear galley, a heavy beverage cart has dislodged from its moorings and rammed the counter/cabinet in its path. Soda cans, dinner trays, drawers, ice cubes, trash, and other items spill onto the floor; the galley partition shifts forward 18 inches. A flight attendant sitting in seat 27C gets scalded by a rain of hot coffee.

The front of the plane is taking the brunt of the crash. The cockpit crew is already dead, just milliseconds into the impact sequence; the nose of the plane, including the cockpit and a flight attendant's jump seat, has crumpled and broken off. The first-class section literally disintegrates as tree trunks pound through the airframe and branches shred the thin aluminum-lithium alloy skin of the fuselage. Much of the energy of the crash is absorbed by this destruction of the front of the plane; that makes the middle and rear sections more survivable.

Outside, the left wing has been torn off. The right wing fuel tanks have been punctured and in a moment, jet fuel will slosh out and onto what's left of the forward fuselage.

The plane continues into a ditch, then smacks into the rise of an embankment, creating several breaks and dents in the fuselage. Sixty percent of the passengers in the front third of the plane are dead, many of the rest there sustain serious injuries—concussions, lost limbs, internal injuries. Three front-section passengers and the flight attendant who was sitting with his back to the shorn-off cockpit section miraculously survive, shaken but virtually unscathed.

Midsection passengers have another problem. Though the passengers were securely fastened by their seat belts, the seats were not built strong enough to withstand the expected forces of impact. Numerous seats have broken loose from the floor—floor attachments and metal frame components have simply snapped like twigs. The seats have piled up toward the front. Some passengers have been crushed, others battered fatally by the heavy, flying chairs.

The same thing has happened to a number of seats in the rear third, creating fatalities there too. Nevertheless, the greatest survival rate is in the rear of the plane and the worst survival rate is in the front.

All cabin lights have gone out, the public address system is not functioning, emergency lights are out. Sections of the cabin floor have buckled and split like pavement in an earthquake.

Fire!

The plane has now come to rest, and you regain your faculties. The cabin is dimly lit by dusklight coming in through the windows and by a subtle, unidentified flickering from outside. The floor is tilted to the left at a sharp angle and debris is strewn everywhere, but you don't really notice it; you just wonder why it's so difficult to walk. Amazingly, the cabin aft of row 5 has remained largely intact. That will hinder your escape, because you are alive—for the moment—inside a long, confining metal tube that is presently on fire. The clock is already running: you have approximately 2 minutes now before fire and smoke overcome passengers and consume the plane.

You unbelt the unconscious child next to you

and lift him. On some unseen meter, your chances of survival have just fallen slightly as you've increased your burden. Guided by human instinct, however, you have chosen to risk *not* making it through your narrow window of escape so that you might save one more life.

Suddenly, a sharp pain knifes through your left arm, which may have been broken by flying debris. But the pain doesn't fully register, and some subconscious command causes you to ignore and endure it to carry the child. You also remain unaware of a deep, bloody gash in your left calf. Because of your injuries, your survival chances index drops again.

You move rearward, feeling your way through the dim cabin, counting off seat rows to the rear exit. You move dispassionately past bodies in seats 24A, 24B, 25B, and 25C—your mind and survival mechanisms have put you on automatic pilot to protect you from potentially debilitating emotions and to get you *out of the plane*. Nevertheless, much of what you experience may come back to haunt you in vivid detail in the weeks and months following the accident, or you may forget it all entirely.

The 19-year-old from seat 20F has gotten to the left rear door but doesn't know how to open it. He is panicking. Other passengers have crowded around waiting for the door to be opened. The floor is slippery with ice cubes, food, and liquids that have spilled from the nearby galley. One man is shouting, "Hurry up! Hurry! We'll be killed." The child you're carrying stirs to consciousness and begins crying.

Just then, light fills the cabin as a bright orange fireball bursts through the fuselage somewhere mid-plane. Without checking to see what was outside, someone had opened an overwing emergency exit door onto a raging inferno. Instead of finding a quick way out, the passenger has let fire find a quicker way *in*. A cloud of thick, acrid smoke races toward you along the ceiling at alarming speed. You had 2 minutes to escape smoke and fire after impact; now you've got only 45 seconds.

"Hurry!"

Something appears to have jammed the door, but the mob has focused on the futile task of opening it and has forgotten there are alternative escape routes.

Maybe you should have gone forward instead of back! Maybe you should try to get through the smoke and out the front now!

Your mind is racing. You begin coughing as the smoke cloud descends, and you instinctively bend down to the fresher air below.

Suddenly the child in your arms points and says, "There!" You look and remember the right side aft exit and move to it, pressing past the crashed beverage cart. You blindly grab for the release lever. Suddenly a flight attendant with a bleeding forehead comes up from behind and pushes you back roughly.

"Stop!" she commands.

You're dumbfounded. Why does she want to keep us from escaping? you wonder. You tense for attack, but her demeanor tells you she knows what she's doing.

She presses her face to the window to check for certain that there is no fire outside the door, then she pushes it open and commences evacuation. Cool fresh air rushes in through the bottom of the opening and smoke pours out of the top.

The floor of the plane is almost at ground level, so you can easily jump the 4 feet without a slide. on landing, your left leg gives way and you drop the child you saved. Now, he and another passenger help *you.* The three of you move away from the burning aircraft and away from the white-hot wall of burning jet fuel that has consumed the left wing and doused the forward fuselage with flames.

Your escape time—1 minute, 22 seconds—gives you a new measure of eternity.

Is It Safe to Fly?

Luckily, just about everyone reading this book will *never* experience the foregoing crash scenario. Chances are, for the rest of your life every single plane you board will take off and land *safely.* Over the last 10 years, the odds—stacked heavily in your favor—were 1 in about 900,000 that you would step onto a fatal flight.

To gain proper perspective, just look at the statistics for U.S. scheduled airlines large and small. From 1976 to 1990:

- 108,065,958 scheduled commercial airline flights took off
- 108,065,144 of these flights (or 99.9992467 percent) landed safely

- 674 flights (0.0006227 percent) were involved in an accident that caused *no fatalities*
- 140 flights (0.0001295 percent) crashed with all or *some* fatalities

But the statistical averages can change significantly when you make more specific comparisons. For example, you've heard the oft-cited statistic that flying is 10 times safer than driving an automobile. That is largely true—*on average*. But if you're a typical low-risk driver—40ish, sober, and wearing a seat belt—you are only 1/1,000th as likely to be killed in a car accident than a high-risk driver, according to *Risk Analysis* magazine. That means good drivers, who may have always suspected as much, can be just as safe in their cars as in the air.

The averages can fool you on the airline side of the equation too. At times, some airlines and some flights are much more dangerous than others. For example, National Safety Council data reveal that in 1987, people who flew commuter airlines were 56 percent *more likely* to die in an accident than were people who drove. Also, a flight under adverse weather conditions or at night is always more risky than a clear skies flight.

At the same time, some airlines have a better safety record than others. As everyone who saw the movie *Rain Man* knows, Australia's Qantas Airlines has never had a fatal accident.

In the area of terrorism, some airlines maintain much tighter security procedures than others, and certain airlines are more likely than others to be the target of a bomb. So even though your odds of running into trouble are very slim, it's still a worthwhile endeavor to improve your personal flight safety margins wherever possible.

Some experts have told us there is nothing travelers can do to reduce their chances of turning up on one of those Associated Press listings of crash victims. But those experts are wrong. In fact, there are 11 important steps passengers can take *right now* to lower their risk of dying in a plane crash. The first four involve travel planning and selection of airline and airport before you book your reservations: they will be covered in this chapter. The remaining seven steps, covered in Chapter 3, will help protect you once you're on the plane.

BOX 2-1

FLIGHT SAFETY CHECKLIST

Before you make reservations . . .

1. Choose your airline carefully.
2. Be cautious about commuter airlines.
3. Take a plane equipped with 16-G seats.
4. Take precautions against possible terrorist threat.

On the plane . . .

5. Sit in the safest section of the plane.
6. Choose an exit/aisle seat.
7. Familiarize yourself with the aircraft.
8. Buy your baby a ticket and a safety seat.
9. Employ precrash planning.
10. Carry a simple crash survival kit.
11. Use your head in crisis.

1. Choose Your Airline Carefully

Are some airlines less safe than others? Yes. As Table 2-1 shows, Eastern, USAir, and Piedmont had accident rates significantly higher than most other major airlines from 1986 to 1990, according to NTSB statistics. TWA, Northwest, and Delta were the safest over the same period.

TABLE 2-1

Airline Safety Record
1986–1989

Ranked best-to-worst, based on total number of accidents per 1 million scheduled flight hours. The accident *rate* takes into account the fact that bigger airlines have more flights in the air each year than smaller carriers and thus a greater exposure to the possibility of an accident.

Airline	Four-year Total Accident Rate (accidents per 1 million scheduled flight hours)	Total Accidents 1986–1989	Fatal Accidents 1986–1989	Four-year Fatal Accident Rate (accidents per 1 million scheduled flight hours)
TWA	0.9	2	0	0.0
Northwest	1.3	4	1	0.3
Delta	1.9	8	1	0.2
Pan Am	2.2	3	2	1.5
United	2.3	11	2	0.4
American	2.6	13	1	0.2
Continental	3.0	10	1	0.3
USAir*	4.2	9	1	0.5
Piedmont*	4.4	7	0	0.0
Eastern*	4.8	12	1	0.4

Source: *Ready for Take-off*, NTSB, RSPA.

*US Air and Piedmont merged operations in 1989.

The information contained in this table is updated regularly in *Ready for Take-off Database*, a quarterly publication. For subscription information, write to: Ready for Take-Off *Database*, P.O. Box 521, Easton, PA 18044-0521.

But finding an airline that will put you up into the skies and bring you back down safely involves more than simply shopping for the safest "brand name." Good and bad airline accident records are not just a matter of luck. They are caused directly by corporate management and its strategic priorities, emphasis on safety, ability to handle finances, attitude toward labor, growth and acquisition plans, and their overall competence running the business. Because those elements change over time at each airline, there is an added dimension to every airline's level of safety: some airlines are safer and some are more dangerous *at certain times.*

Eastern's poor accident record, for example, is surely related at least in part to the internal turmoil the company has experienced for many years—union-busting tactics, mutual labor/management distrust, and poor financial management. Even third-safest Delta went through a dangerous period from 1985 through 1988 because management had fallen down on the job, as we will see shortly.

How can consumers possibly *know* when a particular airline has become a higher risk? Like any living organism in time of stress, airlines send off clearly identifiable warning signals. Here's what to look for:

Danger sign number one is whether or not the airline is making a profit. Be cautious about airlines operating in the red. "We base safety ratings on the profitability of the airline, particularly commuter lines," says Ken Plunkett of the Aviation Safety Institute. "If the airline is strapped for cash, it will likely meet [only] minimum standards of safety. There are no statistics that show [that going above the minimum standards] improves safety, but there are none that show it hurts either." The FAA tends to step up safety inspections at financially troubled airlines. "We want to know how a financially unstable airline is keeping up with maintenance," says FAA spokesman David Duff. If an airline's money troubles worry the FAA, they should concern you, too.

Conventional wisdom argues that no major airline—not even a financially troubled one—would ever sacrifice safety. Incredibly, Eastern Airlines may prove that wisdom wrong. In July 1990 a federal grand jury returned a 60-count indictment against Eastern and nine of its managers on charges that from July 1985 to October 1989 the airline's maintenance operations at JFK, LaGuardia, Atlanta's Hartsfield International, and Miami airports ignored critical maintenance and falsified records in an effort to "keep the aircraft in flight at all costs." The airline was also fined for its actions.

"Thousands of innocent passengers may have been put at risk every day by the criminal actions of these defendants," said U.S. Attorney General Richard Thornburgh.

Eastern's bankruptcy-court appointed trustee Martin Shugrue did not dispute the charges, but said there was no conspiracy and that the problems have all been corrected. (The alleged criminal acts took place before Shugrue took over the airline.)

The warning to consumers about placing their trust and doing business with Eastern was clear. But the indictment should put the public on alert about other airlines. "This action is meant to send a clear signal not just to Eastern but to the entire airline industry," said Andrew Maloney, the U.S. attorney in charge of the case.

Table 2-2 ranks the profitability of the eight major U.S. airlines, based on their 1989 operating profit margins. At the top of the list are well-run companies like Delta and American; bankrupt Eastern, Pan Am and USAir are in the basement.

The FAA increases safety inspections if there are labor/management difficulties. In 1988, says

TABLE 2-2

Profitability of Major U.S. Airlines

Airline	Operating Profit Margin (1989)	1989 Operating Revenues (millions)	1989 Operating Profit (millions)
Delta Air Lines	7.8%	$8,648	$ 677
American (AMR Corp.)	7.3%	$9,961	$ 731
United (UAL Corp.)	4.7%	$9,642	$ 457
Northwest†	4.4%	$6,554	$ 290
Continental	3.2%	$4,944	$ 156
TWA†	0.5%	$4,507	$ 24
USAir Group	−5.4%	$4,205	$−228
Pan Am Corp.	−8.8%	$3,612	$−319
Eastern	−55.7%	$1,552	$−865

Source: Ready for Take-off *Database,* Air Transport Association

†Privately owned.

The information contained in this table is updated regularly in *Ready for Take-off Database,* a quarterly publication. For subscription information, write to: *Ready for Take-off Database,* P.O. Box 521, Easton, PA 18044-0521.

Duff, the FAA stepped up inspections at Eastern Airlines because of the bitter union-management war there.

Danger also increases when an airline is experiencing a period of rapid expansion, either through merger or traffic growth. Boom growth at Air Florida from 1977 through 1981 led up to the crash of Air Florida flight 90 into the 14th Street Bridge and icy Potomac River in Washington, DC, on January 13, 1982. Seventy-four people on board the Boeing 737-222 perished along with four others on the bridge. Only four passengers and one flight attendant (all seated in the rear third of the plane) survived.

The National Transportation Safety Board determined that the probable cause of that accident was flight crew error. Contributing to the accident were a prolonged ground delay and the limited winter operations experience of the flight crew. "The Board believes that the captain of flight 90 missed the seasoning experience normally gained as a first officer as a result of the rapid expansion of Air Florida from 1977 through 1981, wherein pilots were upgrading faster than the industry norm to meet the increasing demands of growing schedules," the NTSB said.

Perhaps the best red-flag warning of an accident waiting to happen is a string of "incidents" and/or accidents experienced by one airline over a relatively short period of time. Such was the case with Delta Air Lines. In June 1987, Delta was involved in a series of highly publicized pilot-related incidents:

• One Delta crew tried to take off from a runway being used by another airline's flight taking off in the opposite direction.

• Another Delta crew inadvertently shut down both engines of a Boeing 767 after takeoff.

• Another Delta flight drifted 60 miles off-course over the Atlantic and came near a Continental Airlines jet.

• At Boston's Logan Airport, a Delta flight landed on the wrong runway.

• In Los Angeles, a Delta plane taxied onto the wrong runway and into the path of a United Airlines jet, which roared just 200 feet overhead.

• And, in perhaps the most incredible incident, a Delta flight landed at the wrong airport. The crew landed at Frankfort, Kentucky, under the mistaken notion they had landed in Lexington, Kentucky, the flight's real destination.

Amusing though some of these incidents may be, when they come in such a short span of time, it's more than mere coincidence; in this case, it indicated big problems inside Delta's flight operations and training programs. FAA inspections found that there were breakdowns in cockpit communications; a lack of crew coordination and lapses of discipline in the cockpit, a lack of definitive guidance from managers responsible for developing cockpit procedures, and a poor training program. In some cases, cockpit crew members didn't know exactly who was responsible for verifying wing flap position (the flaps are what give the plane lift on take-off). In little more than two years—between August 1, 1986 and September 2, 1988, Delta had three accidents and 108 incidents.

Despite warnings from the FAA, Delta management did not adequately address the problems. The FAA, meanwhile, never really cracked down on Delta. On August 31, 1988, Delta flight 1141 crashed on takeoff from Dallas-Ft. Worth airport. Fourteen passengers and crew aboard the Boeing 727-232 died, 76 were injured, and 18 others walked away with only a traumatic memory. You could have seen this accident coming from a mile away: the flight crew took off without the wing flaps and slats properly configured, and a takeoff configuration warning system failed to alert the crew to their mistake. Contributing to the accident were Delta management's slow implementation of necessary changes in operating procedures and training, and the FAA's inability to get Delta in line. This accident also occurred during a period of rapid growth for the airline.

Other major accidents have been foreshadowed by strings of accidents with the same airline. The crash of United flight 232 in Sioux City, Iowa, in July 1989, which killed 111, was preceded by five other United accidents in the short span of a year, starting on June 26, 1988. And in the 21-month period before the crash of a Continental jet at Denver Stapleton Airport in November 1987, which killed 28, Continental had four accidents.

Another way to improve your air safety is to limit international travel to U.S. flag carriers and airlines of the major industrial countries.

According to a 1987 U.S. Defense Department study, the accident rate for U.S. airlines was 1 in 4.4 million flights versus a rate of 1 accident for every 280,000 flights on airlines from South America, Asia, and Africa.

Indian Airlines illustrates the third-world airline problem. After a brand new Indian Airlines Airbus A-320 crashed on landing in Bangalore, India, in February 1990, killing 93, the Indian government was forced to ground the airline's A320-fleet while the Civil Aviation Ministry investigated whether the craft was too sophisticated for the airline's crews. Indeed, according to press reports when the first A-320s were delivered in 1988, Indian Airlines pilots and engineers protested that personnel should be sent to France (where the Airbus planes are manufactured) for proper maintenance training.

Indian Airlines has also suffered a number of strange incidents and accidents in recent years according to *The New York Times*. Among these, one pilot forgot to lower the landing gear before touchdown, a plane crashed into a bull wandering on the runway, and angry passengers commandeered planes.

2. Be Cautious About Commuter Airlines

One of the many results of airline deregulation has been a boom in commuter airline travel. In 1978, 11.3 million passengers flew commuter airlines; 11 years later in 1989, 38 million people flew them, according to the Regional Airline As-

sociation. Sooner or later, you'll likely find yourself on a commuter airplane.

Unfortunately, though safety levels have improved, commuter airlines are still considerably
more accident-prone than the major carriers. From
1979 through 1989, the fatal accident rate for
major airlines was only 0.5 per 1 million departures. Over the same period the fatal accident
rate for commuter airlines was more than six
times greater—3.0 fatal accidents for every 1 million departures.

Commuter airlines are less safe for several
reasons. There is a high turnover rate and consequent lack of experience among pilots on
commuter lines. That's because the best, most
experienced commuter pilots quickly move up to
higher-paying jobs with major airlines, making
commuter operations an unofficial training ground
for the majors. Inexperience has led to passenger
deaths. According to a 1988 General Accounting
Office study, 95 percent of the commuter plane
accidents in 1985 were caused by pilot error.

To improve your personal flight safety, use
caution *whenever* you step outside the major scheduled airline system. The best precaution you can
take—if possible—is to avoid small commuter aircraft with seating for 30 or fewer passengers.
These small commuter planes operate under Part
135 of FAA regulations. Table 2-3 reflects the
safety record of these aircraft.

Larger commuter planes with capacity for 31
or more passengers operate under Part 121 of
FAA regulations, and are as safe as the majors.
The safety record of these large commuter air-

craft is included with that of the majors' big jets in Table 2-4.

How can you tell if you've got reservations on a small commuter aircraft *before* you actually board the plane? Ask the ticket or travel agent what kind of plane is assigned to the flight and how many seats it has. Thirty or fewer seats is the number to avoid if you can. Refer to Table 2-5 for a listing of frequently used small commuter planes.

TABLE 2-3

		Commuter Airline Safety (planes with 30 or fewer seats)	
Year	Fatal Accidents	Total Deaths	Fatal Accidents per 1 Million Departures
1979	15	66	8.0
1980	8	37	4.5
1981	9	32	4.9
1982	5	14	2.5
1983	2	10	0.9
1984	7	46	2.6
1985	7	36	2.7
1986	2	4	0.7
1987	10	57	3.5
1988	2	21	0.7
1989	5	31	1.7
TOTAL	72	354	NA
AVERAGE	7	32	3.0

Source: NTSB.

The information contained in this table is updated regularly in *Ready for Take-off Database*, a quarterly publication. For subscription information, write to: *Ready for Take-off Database*, P.O. Box 521, Easton, PA 18044-0521.

TABLE 2-4

Major Airline Safety
(planes with 31 or more seats)

Year	Fatal Accidents	Total Deaths	Fatal Accidents per 1 Million Departures
1979	4	348	0.7
1980	0	0	0.0
1981	4	2	0.7
1982	4	222	0.6
1983	4	14	0.8
1984	1	4	0.2
1985	4	196	0.7
1986	2	4	0.1
1987	4	229	0.4
1988	3	274	0.3
1989	8	130	1.1
TOTAL	38	1423	NA
AVERAGE	3	129	0.5

Source: NTSB.

The information contained in this table is updated regularly in *Ready for Take-off Database*, a quarterly publication. For subscription information, write to: *Ready for Take-off Database*, P.O. Box 521, Easton, PA 18044-0521.

TABLE 2-5

Small Commuter Planes

Aircraft	Number of Seats
Beech C99 BE-99	15
Beech 1300 Airliner BE-1300	13
Beech 1900 BE-1900	19
British Aerospace Jetstream 31 BAe-3101	19
CASA C212-300	26

continued

Aircraft	Number of Seats
Cessna 402 CE-402	8
Cessna Caravan I CE-208	9
Cessna Caravan II CE-406	12
Commuter Air Transports CATPASS 200-15	13
deHavilland Twin Otter DHC-6	20
Dornier DO-228-212	19
Embraer Brandeirante EMB-110-P1	19
Embraer Brasilia EMB-120	30
Embraer CBA 123	19
Fairchild Metro III SA-227-AC	19
Nomad N22B	12
Nomad II N24A	16
Pilatus B-N Islander BN2B-26, BN2B-20	8
Pilatus B-N Turbine Islander BN2T	8
Piper PA-T1040	9
Shorts 330	30

Source: Regional Airline Association.

Don't automatically assume you'll be on a big jet just because you've booked your flight with a major airline. Sometimes it is difficult to identify a commuter airline because of "code-sharing" arrangements with major carriers. Under a code-sharing agreement, the commuter line does business under a version of the major carrier's name. For example, Crown Airways operates planes under both Parts 135 and 121 and is affiliated with USAir. It does business under the name USAir Express, and if you book a flight with USAir, you may be put on Crown Airways for part of the journey without being told you're not really flying USAir. The major airline benefits by using the commuter line to effectively extend its route system and provide a more extensive service area. Both the commuter and major airline benefit from feeding passengers to each other. (For a listing of the major airlines' code-sharing partners, see Chapter 7.)

Although avoiding small commuter planes will improve your margin of safety, it is not always possible or even practical. If you must fly on a small commuter plane, there are several other safety precautions you can take.

Make sure the plane is a turboprop or turbojet. "The safety statistics are better for turbine engines than for piston-driven propeller craft," says Ed Arbon, a retired pilot who is vice president of the Flight Safety Foundation, a nonprofit organization based in Arlington, VA. Turbojets are easy to identify: they appear to have no propeller blades because they are enclosed inside the engine casing, and they resemble the turbofan engines found on the big airliners. Turboprops and piston-driven propellers are a little trickier to separate because both have big exposed propeller blades.

Commonly used commuter planes powered by piston engines are the Britten Norman B-N Islander, Cessna 206 and 402/404, Convair 440, Douglas DC-3, Martin 404, and Piper Cherokee 6 and Navajo.

Typical turboprop planes are the Beech 1900, British Aerospace Jetstream 31, deHavilland DHC-7 (Dash 7), and DHC-8 (Dash 8), Embraer Brasilia, Fairchild Metro II and III, Fokker F-27, and Shorts SD3-30 and 360.

Another way to reduce your risk when flying a commuter airline is to avoid flying in bad weather or at night. "Sometimes small airplanes don't have all the sophisticated instrumentation they could have for bad weather," says Arbon. "The small airports many commuters use don't have sophisticated bad-weather equipment either, and aren't as well lit as major airports." Darkness and weather are of less concern to big jetliners using large modern airports.

3. Take a Plane Equipped with 16-G Seats

A major cause of death in survivable crashes is failure of the airline seat to stay connected to the floor. "Sixty percent of all accident fatalities are caused by flying debris and seats breaking loose from the floor," says Kenneth Plunkett, a research analyst for the Aviation Safety Institute.

The so-called 9-G seats on most planes flying today are more likely to separate from the floor on impact than newer 16-G seats. (Each "G" equals the force of gravity. With a 1-G force, a 100-pound person would weigh 100 pounds; with a 5-G force, the same 100-pound person would effectively weigh 500 pounds.) In an accident, when the forward force on today's seats exceeds 9 G's, the passenger's head smashes into the tray table and other objects as he and his seat go flying through the cabin. Flying seats also batter and kill the other passengers they hit.

The 16-G seat is more crashworthy because it is designed to withstand 16 gravities of forward force. (Automobile seats, by comparison, can withstand 30 G's of force.) According to the NTSB, the United DC-10 that crashed in Sioux City was *not* equipped with the new 16-G seats. Some of the dead scattered on runways 22 and 31 were held securely in their seats by their seat belts, rescue personnel said, but the seats had broken loose from the floor. The 16-G seat costs just $36 more than the 9-G seat, and the FAA has known about the benefits of 16-G seats for almost 30 years now. But the FAA has dragged its feet and has not yet required that the safer seats be installed.

You can, however, protect yourself from FAA laxity. We surveyed nine major carriers and found that some airlines have begun installing the 16-G seats on their new jets and on planes they're refurbishing. As Table 2-6 shows, American leads the pack with more than 38,350 16-G seats—55 percent of its fleet's seating. Northwest, United, and USAir are also doing a creditable job installing the 16-G seats. United says its refurbishment program will replace every seat in its fleet with 16-G seats by 1995. Eastern and Delta have a few thousand 16-G seats each and Pan Am has a few hundred. Continental has none.

4. Take Precautions Against Possible Terrorist Threat

Your chances of being blown out of the sky or hijacked by terrorists are even smaller than the possibility of your plane crashing. If you travel primarily in the United States, the threat is next to nonexistent. Nevertheless, if you are worried, you *can* take some precautionary steps to reduce the danger even further.

TABLE 2-6

Where to Find the Safest Seats

Airlines ranked best-to-worst in terms of the percentage of 16-G seats making up the airline's total seating.

Airline	Number of 16-G Seats Now in Fleet	16-G Seats as a Percentage of Total Seating
American	38,350	55
Northwest	13,000	25
USAir	10,000	18
United	10,205	14
Eastern	5,018	12
Pan Am	850	4
Delta	2,000	3
Continental	0	0
TWA	NA	NA

Source: *Ready for Take-off Database*, airline data.

The information contained in this table is updated regularly in *Ready for Take-off Database*, a quarterly publication. For subscription information, write to: *Ready for Take-off Database*, P.O. Box 521, Easton, PA 18044-0521.

Start by again choosing your airline carefully. Some airlines are more likely to be targeted than others, says Neil C. Livingstone, a security specialist and author of several books on terrorism. Indian Airlines has been hit by members of the Sikh religious sect and Kuwait Airlines has been the target of Shiite moslems. U.S. airlines traveling internationally have been a favorite for Iranian and Moslem terrorists.

In September 1989, the FAA fined Pan Am $630,000 for security violations at its facilities at Germany's Frankfurt Airport and London's Heathrow Airport. Since the FAA investigation, Pan Am has corrected deficiencies. However, the effectiveness of security is in large part a result of management's commitment to protecting its passengers. At Pan Am that attitude is not entirely clear. In response to the FAA charges, Pan Am Chairman Thomas G. Plaskett said the FAA pointed out problems that were "generally of an administrative rather than substantive nature." As noted earlier, federal investigators had a much less casual view of the situation.

Airlines from countries not embroiled in local conflicts—Sweden, Singapore, Hong Kong, Switzerland—are considered to be safer, says Livingstone. "SAS, Swissair, and Singapore Airlines are three of the best and safest," he says.

In 1987, 30,000 frequent flyers from more than 100 countries were surveyed by the International Foundation of Airline Passengers Associations. Although most airline safety and security activities are carried out behind the scenes and not in full view of passengers, many passengers had definite feelings about the safety consciousness of the airlines they'd recently flown.

Table 2-7 outlines their views. Safety experts (and anyone who has been through EL AL security) agree that EL AL Israel Airlines is the James Bond 007 of airlines. The cargo compartments of EL AL planes are reinforced against explosives, says Livingstone, and when one bomb did explode inside the cargo bay of an EL AL jet in 1972, the plane landed safely. EL AL won't discuss security, but Livingstone says the airline's planes also have missile detection systems and can even fire decoy flares to draw surface-to-air missiles away from the plane.

Every EL AL passenger goes through a security interview, and the interrogators are trained to spot nervous terrorists as well as people unwittingly duped into carrying a bomb on board. This kind of grilling saved the lives of 375 people aboard flight 16 from London to Tel Aviv on April 17, 1986, says Livingstone. During an interview, EL AL security officers suspected, then found, that Anne-Marie Murphy was carrying plastic explosives in her luggage, put there by her fiancé. Unbeknownst to Murphy, her fiancé was a terrorist in the Syrian Abu Nidal group.

Other top-rated airlines were Swissair, Lufthansa, Qantas, and Delta. Pan Am did not make the top 10 list.

TABLE 2-7

World's Most Safety-Conscious Airlines		
Rank	Airline	*Percentage of Recent Users Judging this Airline Most Safety-conscious*
1	EL AL	47
2	Swissair	34
3	Lufthansa	32
4	Qantas	26
5	Delta	23
6	SAA	16
7	Singapore	16
8	American	15
9	SAS	15
10	KLM	14

Source: International Foundation of Airline Passengers Associations.

BOX 2-2

HOW GOOD IS YOUR AIRPORT SECURITY?

When sizing up security, you should also choose your airport carefully. Because airports are an entry point for terrorists and because some states sponsor or tacitly encourage terrorism, some are at higher risk of terrorist infiltration than others.

With U.S. involvement in the Persian Gulf, you are at highest risk flying to and from airports in Saudi Arabia, Egypt, and the United Arab Emirates. Security at airports in the poor third-world countries of Asia and Africa "is no more than cosmetic," says Paul Wilkinson, an expert on international terrorism.

Security specialists say the most dangerous airports in Europe are Athens and Frankfurt. A study of Athens airport by EL AL security found that sophisticated bomb equipment was not being used, security personnel were incompetent, and the Greek government was unwilling to fight terrorists.

In the United States, the FAA does a confidential rating of airport security. In 1989 Livingstone identified the 16 U.S. airports most vulnerable to terrorist attack that he learned were on the FAA's secret list: Atlanta's Hartsfield, Baltimore-Washington International, Boston's Logan International, Chicago's O'Hare, Dallas-Ft. Worth, Denver Stapleton, Detroit Metropolitan, Honolulu, Houston Intercontinental, Los Angeles, Miami, New York's JFK, San Francisco, San Juan, and Washington's Dulles and National airports.

Yet another way to separate the safer from the less safe airports is to look at which have the latest bomb-detection equipment. The thermal neutron analysis detector has a 95 percent success rate in spotting all types of explosives, including the increasingly popular Czech-made Semtex plastic explosive. Today's airport X-ray machines can miss plastic explosives.

Table 2-8 shows which airports and airlines presently have or are expected to get the 20-ton, $1 million TNA machines. The FAA is still gathering data on the TNA, and a planned deployment of hundreds of the machines worldwide has been delayed.

TABLE 2-8

Who Has or Expects The Latest Bomb Detection Technology?

Airport	Airline
Baltimore-Washington International (E)	NA
Frankfurt-Main Airport, West Germany (E)	Pan Am
Gatwick Airport, London	All U.S. airlines
John F. Kennedy International Airport, New York	TWA
Miami International Airport	Pan Am
Washington Dulles International Airport	United

Source: FAA.

E = Expected here, according to informed sources and reports.

The information in this table is updated regularly in *Ready for Take-off Database*, a quarterly publication. For subscription information, write to: *Ready for Take-off Database*, P.O. Box 521, Easton, PA 18044-0521.

CHAPTER 3

Personal Air Safety—Part II

How to Protect Yourself on the Plane

The job of protecting yourself from air crashes, unsafe airlines, and terrorists does not end after you've finished your travel planning and have thoughtfully selected both airline and airport. There is still much more you can do to improve your personal air safety once you're on the plane.

5. Sit in the Safest Section of the Plane

The National Transportation Safety Board and other experts deny that where you're seated in a crashing plane plays a role in your chance for survival. They say the Grim Reaper chooses who dies on a case-by-case basis, depending on such unpredictable factors as which part of the plane hits the ground first, how the plane impacts, and the terrain and structures the plane crashes into. You can't pick a safe seat with any certainty, they argue, because you can't predict how the plane will hit.

There is a certain amount of truth to this, and

indeed you cannot pick a 100 percent guaranteed survivor's seat. But this fact ignores another fact— that some areas of the plane are statistically *more likely* to produce fatalities than others, in much the same way the front, so-called suicide seats, of an automobile are more dangerous than the backseats in an accident. Because an airplane, like a car, usually crashes while moving in a forward direction, the front end can be expected to bear the brunt of a disproportionately high number of impacts. A plane is rarely rear-ended in midair, nor is it likely to back into a crash tail-first (though the tail *can* hit ground first, particularly on takeoff). Safety experts have a macabre joke about this: the pilot is always the first one to arrive at the scene of an accident.

Although the experts were absolutely certain no part of a plane is safer than another, none could cite statistical evidence to support this claim. Indeed, we've found no study available to the public that uses an unbiased statistical body count to determine how seat location affects a passenger's chances of surviving a crash. One source inside the NTSB, busily using colored pencils to diagram the seat location of survivors and fatalities in one accident, said the Board hasn't really put all the seating diagrams side-by-side to find a pattern. "We kind of deal with each accident on a case-by-case basis," she admitted.

So *we* dug out the evidence and put the diagrams side by side, a time-consuming process that involved poring through hundreds of NTSB accident reports, thousands of pages of supporting documents, and in one case, a handwritten

seating chart of survivors and fatalities sketched
out by an investigator while talking to a crash
survivor. The detailed accident reports covered
U.S. common carrier and commuter airline accidents for the last 12 years. We eliminated crashes
that did not yield both survivors *and* fatalities,
because crashes with either all survivors or all
fatalities make seating location a moot point. For
example, American Airlines flight 191, the DC-
10-10 whose left engine broke off on takeoff at
Chicago O'Hare in May 1979, and sent the plane
nosediving into the ground, killed all 271 people
on board.

We also eliminated reports that provided in-
sufficient data about where the survivors and
fatalities were sitting. Finally, we threw out a
handful of unusual accidents. For instance, in
June 1983, the Air Canada DC-9 that caught fire
in-flight and then landed in Cincinnati was atypical, in that the plane did not crash and flight
attendants had directed passengers to move forward, away from the fire in the rear lavatory.
Aloha Airlines flight 243, during which 18 feet
of the forward fuselage skin peeled off in-flight,
sweeping one flight attendant out of the plane
and to her death, was also unusual. And the
crash of a Lockheed Learstar L-18 near Silvana,
Washington, in August 1983, which killed 11 of
the 26 on board had to be discarded because of
the unique survival factors, as explained in the
NTSB report: ". . . because the occupants were
parachutists, several were able to leave the airplane before it crashed and descended safely by
parachute."

We were left with data from 18 accidents on which we could fairly base a conclusion. Half of the crashes involved large airliners, the rest involved smaller commuter planes. Each plane's passenger cabin was divided into thirds, based on the number of rows in the plane, and the survival rate in each section was calculated. Where the number of rows didn't divide evenly by three, the appropriate fraction of fatalities and survivors in borderline seats was apportioned to each section. For example, in Chart 3-1, the dividing line between the front and middle third of the cabin falls at row 12.7, where seven fatalities were seated. So 7/10 of each fatality were placed in the front third and 3/10 were placed in the middle third. The 7 fatalities were thus split: 4.9 to the front third and 2.1 to the middle third.

The data show a clear-cut pattern: occupants in the front of the plane had the lowest survival rate on average, and the rate of survival increased as one moved toward the rear of the plane. On average in the crashes we studied, *passengers were 34 percent safer in the rear third of the plane* than they were in the front third. In the 18 accidents, the survival rates averaged 44 percent for the front third, 47 percent for the middle third, and 59 percent for the rear third. The worst survival rate—an average of just 34 percent—was in the front-most part of the plane, the cockpit.

To fully understand the survival pattern and to see how fickle fate can be, one must examine some of the individual accidents more closely.

Case 1: Delta Air Lines Flight 191

The crash of Delta flight 191, a big Lockheed
L-1011-385-1, illustrates the classic survival rate
pattern. The survival rate in the cockpit and
front third was zero, a better 12 percent in the
middle third, and the highest, 50 percent, in the
rear third. (Note that survival rates are the *percentage of people in each section* who survived
and not the percentage distribution of total survivors throughout the plane.)

Flight 191 crashed while attempting to land at
Dallas-Ft. Worth Airport on August 2, 1985 at
6:05 P.M. Weather: rain, thunderstorm. Killed: 134
passengers and crew members; 26 passengers and
3 flight attendants survived. (Flight 191 is dubbed
Delta Dallas I by crash experts, because another
Delta jetliner crashed at the same airport in the
same month three years later—Delta Dallas II.)

The Delta Dallas I crash occurred when the
aircraft was hit by a microburst or wind shear—a
strong downward gust. The jet hit a car on Texas
State Highway 114, then plowed through two
airport water tanks. The impact with the water
tanks played a major role in creating fatalities
and demonstrates how the front typically absorbs
the brunt of impact with ground objects. Because
of that impact, all but the aft section of the
fuselage disintegrated, and a severe fire erupted.
Indeed, the NTSB concluded the impact sequence
was not survivable for passengers forward of row
40 (row 32 on our chart)—even though 12 *did*
survive. For passengers in row 40 and back, the
crash *was* survivable, the NTSB determined.

CHART 3-1

Cockpit Survive:	0.0	**Delta Flight 191**
Fatal:	3.0	
Survival Rate:	0%	

F*
⟵ EXIT

Front section (Rows 1–6) — F* EXIT ⟶ at right

ROW	A	B	C	D	E	F
1	A	B	—	—	E	F
2	F	_	F	F	F	F
3	F	F	—	—	F	F
4	F	F	—	—	_	F
5	F	F	—	—	F	F
6	F	F	F	_	_	F

Front Third		
(Rows 1–12.7)		
Survive:	0.0	
Fatal:	54.9	
Survival Rate:	0%	

Rows 7–26

ROW	A	B	C	D	E	F	G	H	J
7	F	_	F	_	_	F	F	F	F
8	F	F	_	_	_	_	_	F	F
9	_	F	_	_	_	_	F	F	F
10	F	_	F	_	_	_	F	F	F
11	_	_	F	F	F	_	_	F	F
12	F	F	F	_	_	_	F	_	_
13	F	F	F	_	_	F	F	F	F

F*
⟵ EXIT   F* EXIT ⟶

Middle Third		
(Rows 12.7–25.4)		
Survive:	7.0	
Fatal:	51.1	
Survival Rate:	12%	

ROW	A	B	C	D	E	F	G	H	J
14	F	_						_	_
15	F	F	F	F	F	F	F	F	S
16	F	F	F	_	F	_	F	F	F
17	F	F	_	_	_	_	F	F	F
18	F	F	F	_	_	_	_	_	_
19	F	F	F	F	_	_	_	F	_
20	F	F	_	_	_	_	F	F	F
21	S	F	_	_	_	_	_	_	F
22	F	_	F	_	_	_	_	_	F
23	_	_	S	_	_	_	_	_	_
24	_	_	S	_	_	F	F	F	_
25	_	S	F	F	F	_	F	S	S
26	F	F	_	_	_	F	F	F	_

continued

```
                        27  _ _   _ _ _ _ _   S F
        Rear Third      28  F F   _ _ _ _ _   _ _
      (Rows 25.4–38)    29  F _   _ _ _ _ _   _ S
      Survive:   21.0   30  F F F _ _ F _   _ F
        Fatal:   21.0   31  S F   _ _ _ _ _   S F
   Survival Rate:  50%          F*              S*
                            <—— EXIT        EXIT ——>
                        32  _ S             _ _
    F = Fatality        33  F _   _ _ _ _ _   S S
    S = Survivor        34  _ F   _ _ _ _ _   S S
    _ = Unoccupied Seat 35  F F   _ _ S _   S S
 <—— = Emergency Exit   36  F F   S S _ S   _ S
    * = Flight Attendant 37  _ _   _ _ _ _   S _
                        38  <—EXIT  S _ _ _   EXIT——>
                                S*              S*
```

Case 2: Downeast Airlines Flight 46

The crash of Downeast Airlines Flight 46, a deHavilland DHC-6-200, shows that the rearward sections can be safer in small planes too. The DHC-6-200, an 18-passenger plane, crashed into a heavily wooded area little more than a mile south of Knox County Regional Airport in Rockland, Maine, during an instrument approach at about 9 P.M. on May 30, 1979. Weather: fog, conditions deteriorating.

The aircraft smashed through trees, but did not burn. The forward 5 feet of the 18-foot passenger cabin were completely destroyed. The 17 persons killed died from impact trauma to the head and chest, and most suffered internal injuries as well. One passenger, sitting on the borderline between the middle and rear third of the

CHART 3-2

				A	B C
Cockpit Survive:	0.0		**Downeast Airlines**		
Fatal:	2.0		**Flight 46**		
Survival Rate:	0%				
				A	B C
Front Third (Rows 1–2.3) ←	1			F	_ F→
Survive:	0.0				
Fatal:	5.9	2		F	F F
Survival Rate:	0%				
		3		F	F F
Middle Third (Rows 2.3–4.6)					
Survive:	.6	4		F	F F
Fatal:	5.7				
—Survival Rate:	10%	5			F S
Rear Third (Rows 4.6–7)		6			F
Survive:	.4		←—EXIT—→		
Fatal:	3.4	7		F	_ F
Survival Rate:	11%				

F = Fatality
S = Survivor
_ = Unoccupied Seat
← = Emergency Exit

Source: NTSB.

plane, survived and escaped the wreckage with a deep scalp wound and leg and wrist fractures. No one in the cockpit or front third survived.

Case 3: Continental Airlines Flight 1713

Although front section cabin seating *tends* to be more dangerous, the crash of another big jet, Continental Airlines Flight 1713, a McDonnell Douglas DC-9-14, shows that the front is not universally the most dangerous. Flight 1713 crashed on takeoff at Denver's Stapleton International Airport on November 15, 1987, at 2:15 P.M. Weather: moderate snow and fog; temperature, 28 degrees. The aircraft had not been deiced a second time after a departure delay. Ice on the wings caused the pilot to lose control of the plane. On impact a fireball was seen, but there was no major fire afterward.

Again, the cockpit crew was killed. The rear was again the safest section to be in, with a 93 percent survival rate. But the midsection of the plane had a lower survival rate—46 percent—than the front third's 60 percent, because of the way the plane crumpled: the forward part of the fuselage came to rest on its left side; the aft section of the fuselage was twisted upside down. This contortion caused part of the middle section to become crushed like a discarded aluminum can, bringing the ceiling and floor to within inches of each other. Twenty-five passengers and three crew members were killed by traumatic impact injuries or mechanical asphyxia—being crushed. Fifty-two passengers and two flight attendants survived. Again, note that the rear third was the safest place to sit.

Case 4: United Airlines Flight 232

Don't fail to note this important caveat about seat location: if you sit in the rear third, you *can* still get killed in an accident. For example, sitting in the rear third of the plane didn't help two passengers on USAir Flight 5050, a Boeing 737-400, which crashed on takeoff at LaGuardia

Airport in New York on the evening of September 20, 1989. The only two fatalities in that accident were in the rear third, at the point where the fuselage broke open. (Full seating location information for that accident was unavailable as *Ready for Take-off* went to press.)

Nor was rear-section seating a guarantee for survival on United Airlines flight 232, the DC-10 that crashed at Sioux Gateway Airport in Iowa on the afternoon of July 19, 1989. Weather: clear. The aircraft became disabled in-flight when a microscopic flaw in an engine disk caused the tail engine to explode. That severed hydraulic lines used to control the craft's ailerons, elevators, rudder, and flaps. Nevertheless, Captain Alfred C. Haynes (and flight crew members Dudley Dvorak, William Records, and Dennis Fitch) managed to pilot the jet to a crash landing at the Sioux City airport. On touchdown, however, the plane cartwheeled into a fiery wreck captured on videotape by a local TV news camera crew. As the fuselage tumbled, the front *and* rear sections disintegrated. A large chunk of fuselage—made up of half the front section and half the midsection of the plane—remained largely intact. Amazingly, 184 on board survived while 112 others died.

Despite what we said earlier about the rarity of planes "backing into" an accident, that was the effect of the cartwheeling in this highly unusual impact. The typical survival rate pattern was thus completely reversed: incredibly, the highest survival rate was in the cockpit, where 100 percent of the four-man crew survived. The

CHART 3-4

Cockpit Survive:	4.0				
Fatal:	0.0		**United Airlines**		
Survival Rate:	100%		**Flight 232**		

			S* S*			F*
Front Third			←EXIT			EXIT→
(Rows 1–11.7)			A B	C D	E F	
Survive:	71.3	1	F F	F F	F F	
Fatal:	20.0	2	F F	F F	S S	
Survival Rate:	78%	3	F F	F F	S _	
		4	F F	S F	F S	
		5	S S		S _	

			S*			S*
			←EXIT			EXIT→
			A B	C D E F G	H J	
		6	S S	S _ S _ S	S S	
		7	S S	S S S S S	S S	
		8	S S	S S SSS _#	S S	
		9	SSS#S	S S S S	S S	
		10	S S	S S S S S	S S	
		11	F S	S S S S S	#S SS	
		12	S S	S S S S S	S S	
		13	S S	S F S S S	S S	
		14	S S	S S S S S	S S	
Middle Third		15	S S	S S S S S	S S	
(Rows 11.7–23.4)		16	S S	S S S S S	S S	
Survive:	72.9	17	S S	S S S S _	S S	
Fatal:	26.0	18	S *S	S S S S	S*	
Survival Rate:	74%		←EXIT			EXIT→
		19		F F SFS S#		
		20	F F	F F S S S	S S	
		21	F F	F F F S S	S S	
		22	F F	F F F S S	S S	
		23	F F	F F S F S	S F	
		24	F F	F F _ S S	F S	

continued

```
                        25   F F  F F S S    S F
                        26   F S S S F F F    F F
        Rear Third      27   F F F S F F S    F F
     (Rows 23.4–35)     28   F F — F F S F    F F
        Survive:  35.8  29   S F F F F S      F F
          Fatal:  65.0  30   F S S F S S F    F F
    Survival Rate:  36% 31   S F F F — F      F F
                        32   F S F F F F F    F F
                        33   F F   F F F F    F S
                        34   S S   S S F S    F S
                        35   S S   S S S S    F S

 F = Fatality                     S*          S*
 S = Survivor             <———EXIT      EXIT———>
 — = Unoccupied Seat
 * = Flight Attendant
 # In-lap infants in seats 8E, 9B, 11J, and 19E
```

Source: NTSB.

next-best rate was in the front third with 78
percent of passengers there surviving. In the middle third, a slightly lower 74 percent survived.
The rear third experienced the worst rate of
survival—just 36 percent. Unusual as this survival rate pattern is, it happens.

Our study sample is, of course, relatively small.
Statistical experts know that small sample sizes
can distort conclusions because the selection
process may gather a sample that does not reflect
the true averages of the larger population. For
several reasons, however, we do not believe that
sample size prejudices our findings.

First, the sample size is small not by our choice
but because fatal airline accidents are a relatively rare occurrence. Our "sample" represents

100 percent of U.S. accidents fitting the criteria of study (significant accidents with *both* fatalities and survivors and availability of data). Nor is sample selection biased by limitations within *our* control. Finally, the sample is drawn from accidents that occurred over a lengthy time span, which should tend to reduce statistical bias that can result from looking at only a narrow snapshot (one-year, five-year) of accidents.

Theoretically, despite all this, the number of survivor-and-fatality accidents that have occurred over the past 12 years may still be considered small—relative to the larger population of accidents over all future time *that have not yet occurred.* Consequently, consider this study only the best available guidance to date; *Ready for Take-off* will continue to gather data on future accidents and report updated results in any subsequent editions.

6. Choose an Exit/Aisle Seat

Although rear seating is an important survival factor, don't blindly ask for the seat farthest to the rear of the plane. There may be no close exit for you to escape through quickly if you survive impact. Always be mindful of the exits *before* you get on the plane and choose an aisle seat as close as possible to a door or emergency exit. Why? "Fire and smoke are the biggest problems in survivable crashes," says Van Gowdy, manager of the biodynamic section of the FAA's Civil Aeromedical Institute in Oklahoma City. "In case of fire, I'd like to be sitting close to an exit."

John Galipault, a pilot and former jet navigator who is president of the Aviation Safety Institute, an independent nonprofit research company based in Worthington, Ohio, tries to sit not only near an exit but on the aisle, so he can see what's going on in the cabin after a crash. The aisle seat also affords instant access to escape routes. "I don't want to be in a window seat with a 400-pound guy next to me; that guy isn't going to be moving after impact, and I'm going to have to climb over him," says Galipault.

A number of planes don't have an extreme rear exit. The deHavilland DASH-8, for example, a 37-seater popular with commuter airlines, has no rear exit leading directly outside. If you're seated in the back row—row 9—your closest exit is the left or right emergency door on row 4.

Among larger planes, the Boeing 727-100 has a tail air-stair exit, but no rear *side* exits. This provides poor egress in case of an emergency. Flight attendants are trained that this exit *may not be usable* following a "gear-up" landing in which the landing gears break off on impact, don't come down, or sink into soft ground. In that case, the airplane would be resting on its fuselage, and the air stair probably couldn't be opened. Thus, if the tail exit is out of commission for whatever reason, a passenger in row 25 has to make it all the way to the emergency exits at rows 16 and 14. A newer model of the B-727—the B-727-200—on the other hand, *does* have left and right rear exit doors as well as the tail exit.

Among other planes with poor or nonexistent extreme rear exiting according to Airline Seating Guide diagrams: the British Aerospace BAC 1-11,

Fokker F.28-1000, F. 28-3000, F.28-4000, and F-100; McDonnell Douglas DC-9 series; and the Soviet industry Ilyushin Il-62, Tupolev Tu-134, and Yakovlev Yak-42.

Another way to assess the safety of an airplane is to compare the number of seats to the number of emergency exits. The FAA mandates that aircraft have sufficient exiting to evacuate everyone on board in 90 seconds or less. With testing and analysis, a maximum seating capacity is established for each craft. Airlines can then pack on as many seats as possible up to this limit.

But when you understand how the FAA and manufacturers determine what's safe, it becomes clear you should prefer a plane that *doesn't* shoehorn seating right to the limit.

Using real people, manufacturers show that each aircraft model can be evacuated in 90 seconds under nighttime conditions and with half the exits disabled. Numerous other conditions add difficulty—the "passengers" may not be crewmembers or training personnel, and carry-on bags and pillows are thrown into the aisles to create minor obstacles.

But test conditions create a scenario that more closely resembles a mere hard-landing *incident* rather than a real accident: First, the plane is level and resting on all landing gear, rather than in one of two not uncommon crash positions— upside down or precariously tilted. Second, all passengers are alert, able, and ready, rather than confused, injured, and panicked. Third, the plane's emergency lighting—which can be disabled in an accident—remains on. Fourth, a "representative" passenger load is used rather than a full planeload. Fifth, there is no smoke or fire. And, sixth, major obstructions—collapsed overhead bins, displaced partitions or other wreckage—do not hinder escape.

All of these things slow down *real* evacuations. To protect yourself better, any plane you fly should have an extra evacuation safety margin—*fewer* seats than the maximum allowed. The wider the difference between the FAA maximum and the actual number of seats, the better. Many airliners give you a substantial extra exiting edge; others just meet the bare bones requirements.

To learn which planes give you the greatest advantage, we dug out maximum passenger capacity information from type certificate data sheets on file with the FAA. Next, we examined hundreds of diagrams in the *Airline Seating Guide* to learn how many seats U.S. and foreign carriers put into each type aircraft. We then compared the government standards to actual seating and calculated the evacuation safety margins.

The 737-300, for example, is allowed to have up to 149 seats, but United Airlines only installs 128 seats. That 21-seat difference gives United passengers a 14 percent extra safety margin because fewer passengers must make it through the exits. America West, on the other hand, packs 143 seats onto the same plane with the same number of exits. The plane still meets FAA standards, but the 6-seat difference gives passengers only a 4 percent extra safety margin.

As Table 3-1 shows, wide-body planes like the Boeing 747, DC-10, and L-1011 provide the largest

TABLE 3-1

Extra Evacuation Safety Margin

Ranked best-to-worst based on the "Extra Evacuation Safety Margin"—the percentage difference between the actual number of seats on the plane and the maximum number allowed. A plane that is allowed to have, say, 120 seats but only has 110, has an 8% extra safety margin, meaning it has 8% *fewer* seats than allowed. The higher the margin the better. If the same plane had 120 seats, its extra safety margin would be zero. Because seat configurations and numbers vary from airline to airline, we show the average, lowest, and highest margins found for each model among major U.S. and foreign carriers. The ranking is based on the average margin.

| Rank | Aircraft | Extra Evacuation Safety Margin | | |
		Average	Lowest	Highest
1	747-400	39%	25%	46%
2	DC-10	32	18	44
3	747	30	10	57
4	L-1011	29	13	39
5	A310	28	19	38
6	A300	27	21	37
7	747-200	27	7	49
8	DC-8-62, -63, -71	27	6	53
9	767-200	25	18	36
10	MD-81, -82, -83, -88	21	9	35
11	A320	20	16	24
12	757	19	13	28
13	737-300	15	4	26
14	DC-9-51	13	12	14
15	727-200	12	3	20
16	737-200	10	5	18
17	Dash-8	8	8	8
18	Dash-7	7	7	7
19	727-100	4	0	13

Source: *Ready for Take-off*, derived from FAA data and information in the Airline Seating Guide

safety margins. At the other extreme, the Boeing
727-100 offers little more than the minimum exiting capacity for the number of seats airlines tend
to pack on board. The 727-200 is also toward the
bottom of the ratings. Yet the 727 is the most
common model in the U.S. airliner fleet, with
more than 1,100 in active service.

Ironically, several years ago, airlines asked
Boeing Corporation to block the two overwing
exits on its top-rated 747 model so they could
use the exit space for more revenue-producing
seats. That meant a 747 with 434 seats would
have been just a shade over FAA standards; the
8 exits (instead of 10) could evacuate 440 seats.
The Association of Flight Attendants, however,
fought the move, arguing that the blocked exits
would create a 72-foot exitless space in the middle of the plane. "In actual crashes of 747s with
the full 10 exits, there had been a lot of exit
failures and passengers had trouble getting out,"
says Matt Finucane, the AFA's director of Air
Safety and Health Issues. In 1986, the FAA was
forced to prohibit removal of the overwing exits
by limiting the distance between exits to 60 feet.

That rule applies only to U.S. carriers, though.
Foreign airlines *can* block the exits, and some
airlines have eliminated them on some of their
747s. "I got on a British Airways 747, walked
down that long corridor, and saw the overwing
exits were no longer there," says Cindy Yeast, a
U.S. flight attendant and spokesperson for the
AFA. "You just know if the airplane were full
and you had to evacuate it, there's no way you'd
get all those people off before they started falling
over and dying from the smoke."

That is not overdramatization. Adequate exit access on *every* kind of plane saves lives. Two airline accidents involving fire prove it.

Case 5: Northwest Airlink Flight 2268

Close proximity to exits saved the lives of 10 people on Northwest Airlink flight 2268, a tiny 22-passenger CASA C-212-CC, which crashed on landing at Detroit Metropolitan Wayne County Airport on March 4, 1987, at 2:30 P.M. Weather: clear. Seven passengers and 2 crew were killed; 10 others in the plane survived with minor injuries and burns.

The plane landed off the mark and hit a concrete apron to the left of the runway, skidded 398 feet, struck three ground support vehicles, and caught fire. During the impact sequence, the plane flipped over. The fire was extinguished within 2 minutes of the first alarm, but because fire and smoke consumed the cabin so rapidly, seven of the upside-down, disoriented passengers were overcome before they could escape.

Although the cockpit took the brunt of the impact and the nose was flattened like a pancake, the pilot and copilot died, as did the passengers, from smoke inhalation and toxic fumes, including cyanide—not from impact trauma. The seats on the plane did not have fire-blocking material that slows down the spread of fire. That would have given passengers at least 40 extra seconds to escape.

The survivors of flight 2268 escaped through

the front emergency exit, opened by a flight attendant, and the rear main exit door, which sprang open on impact. The right side emergency exits were never opened. Look at Chart 3-5 and you'll see the pattern: most of the people closest to the exits made it out alive. The big main exit

CHART 3-5

Cockpit Survive:	0.0				
Fatal:	2.0	**Northwest Airlink**			
Survival Rate:	0%	**Flight 2268**			
		$\longleftarrow$ S*	B	C	$\longrightarrow$
Front Third		1 A	F	_	
(Rows 1–2.7)					
Survive:	3.7	2 S	S	_	
Fatal:	2.4				
Survival Rate:	61%	3 S	F	F	
Middle Third		4 F	S	_	
(Rows 2.7–5.4)					
Survive:	1.7	5 F	_	F	
Fatal:	4.0				
Survival Rate:	30%	6 F	_	S	
Rear Third		7 S	S	S	
(Rows 5.4–8)		8 $\longleftarrow$ EXITS $\longrightarrow$			
Survive:	4.6%				
Fatal:	.6				
Survival Rate:	88%				

F = Fatality
S = Survivor
* = Flight Attendant
_ = Unoccupied Seat
$\longleftarrow$ = Emergency Exit

Source: NTSB.

was at row 8 and the survival rate at row 8 was 100 percent; at row 7, 100 percent again; at row 6, 50 percent, but by row 5 it dropped to 0 percent. In a hellishly fierce aircraft fire, the difference between life and death can be measured in feet.

The pattern is less perfect for the front rows, but it shows nonetheless that proximity to the exit was a lifesaver. Survivors here exited through the smaller front emergency exit. The survival rate for the flight attendant seated right near the exit was 100 percent, but at row 1, it dropped to 0 percent. In row 2 the rate climbed back to 100 percent, then at row 3 it dropped to 33 percent. In row 4 the rate was 50 percent, and in row 5 again, 0 percent.

Case 6: Delta Air Lines Flight 1141

Delta flight 1141, a Boeing 727-232, crashed while taking off from Dallas-Ft. Worth Airport on August 31, 1988, at 9 A.M. Weather: clear. The NTSB concluded that the flight crew had not properly configured the wing flaps and slats for takeoff and an electronic warning system failed to alert the pilot to the mistake. On takeoff, the plane's nose rose at too sharp an angle and the tail hit the runway with a shower of sparks and flame. The wings wobbled from side to side and 650 feet after the first skid, the right wing tip hit the side of the runway, setting the tail afire. The plane then destroyed an ILS (Instrument Landing System) localizer antenna, remained airborne for another 400 feet, then came crashing down. The fuselage—largely intact, though broken open at several points—slid sideways until it came to rest several hundred feet later. Twelve passengers and two flight attendants were killed in this crash, nicknamed Delta Dallas II by investigators because it was the second Delta crash at DFW in three years. The cockpit crew survived, together with 89 passengers and 2 flight attendants.

When the plane came to rest, everyone had survived without debilitating impact trauma injuries. The plane had nine exits, but note how even this large number was significantly reduced: because of fire on the right side of the plane, the big main exit doors on the front and aft right side of the plane were unusable, together with the two right overwing emergency exits. With the fuselage resting on the ground, the rear airstair door was also out of commission. The left aft door was jammed and inoperable. With six of nine doors—67 percent—out of service, passengers had only the forward left service door and the two left overwing emergency exits.

Passengers were lucky to have had a generous amount of time to evacuate the forward cabin—4 minutes and 20 seconds—before fire made it unsurvivable. Aft cabin passengers had considerably less time to escape the fire, because that's where it was burning, up from the cargo area below. Fortunately for the survivors, there were breaks and holes in the fuselage; 47 passengers escaped through these holes. Only 36 survivors used the exits (2 used the front exit, 15 the left forward overwing exit, and 19 the left aft overwing exit). It is not known how 6 others exited.

Eleven of the 14 fatalities made the mistake of heading for the aft service door to escape. Almost a dozen other passengers seated near some of these 11 had escaped by going in the opposite direction and through a break in the fuselage. Unfortunately for those bound for the rear door, the impact of the crash had knocked that door out of alignment with its frame, jamming it closed. By the time the passengers realized this, fire was entering the fuselage break that the others had escaped through, thus sealing off their last escape option.

None of the passengers died of impact trauma. One passenger who had successfully escaped but returned to the plane—possibly to help save others—died of burns 11 days after the accident. The rest died of smoke inhalation.

CHART 3-6

Cockpit Survive:	3.0					
Fatal:	0.0		**Delta Air Lines**			
Survival Rate:	100%		**Flight 1141**			

			S*	S*		
			←—EXIT			
			A	B	EXIT—→	
Front Third		1	S	S	C D	
(Rows 1–9.7)		2	S	S	S S	
Survive:	37.4	3	S	S	S S	
Fatal:	1.4	4	S	S		
Survival Rate:	96%		A B C	D E F		
		5	S S S	S – S		
		6	S S S	S S S		
		7	S – S	S S S		

continued

```
                         8   S _ _   S _ S
                         9   S _ S   _ _ S
─────────────────       10  S _ F   F _ S ───────
                         11  S _ S   _ _ _
    Middle Third         12  S S S   _ S S
  (Rows 9.7–19.4)        13  S S _   _ S S
      Survive:   36.4    14  S _ S   _ _ S
        Fatal:    .6   ← 15  S S S   S _ S →
  Survival Rate:  98%    16  S _ S   _ _ S
                       ← 17  _ _ S   S _ _ →
                         18  S SSS#S _ S
                         19  S _ S   S S S
─────────────────       20  _ _ S   S _ _ ───────
                         21  S _ _   S S S
     Rear Third          22  S _ S   S _ _
  (Rows 19.4–29)         23  F _ S   S _ S
      Survive:   14.2    24  S S F   F _ S
        Fatal:   12.0    25  F _ _   F F _
  Survival Rate:  54%    26          F _ _
                         27 ←── EXIT _ _ EXIT ──→
                         28          _ _ _
                         29      + FF_ F
                                F* F *
                                EXIT
```

───

F = Fatality
S = Survivor
_ = Unoccupied Seat
←── = Emergency Exit
* Flight Attendant
# Infant with passenger in seat 18B
+ Infant with passenger in seat 29D

───

Source: NTSB.

7. Familiarize Yourself with the Aircraft

As soon as you settle into your seat, pull out the plastic card located in the seat pocket in front of you. It shows the plane's layout, location of emergency exits, and how to operate exit releases, inflatable escape chutes, and life rafts. It also shows where fire extinguishers, axes, and flotation devices are located.

Don't ignore this elementary exercise because you think you're already familiar with, say, the Boeing 747. There are four different models of this long-haul plane—the 747-100, 747-200, 747-300, and 747-400. Some of these come in all-passenger versions, a passenger/cargo setup, or a convertible passenger or cargo.

The standard 230-foot-long 747 can carry 300 to 400 seats and has 8 to 10 exits, whereas the smaller 184-foot-long 747SP generally holds 200 to 250 seats and has only 8 exits. Neither have exterior emergency exits in the upstairs section. Both the 747-300 and 747-400, conversely, have stretch upstairs sections and exterior emergency exits from there.

Blasé passengers unnecessarily reduce their chances of survival. When the Association of Flight Attendants gave 800 people who had flown within the past year a 10-question quiz on some of the most rudimentary airplane safety facts, the average grade was an F, with only 55 percent of the answers correct. The questions involved such heard-it-all-before subjects as the use of oxygen masks, emergency exiting, location of flotation devices, and smoking.

Look around the cabin before the plane pushes away from the gate, and locate two to four of your closest exits. Map out your escape route *now*, because an accident can happen at anytime—especially on takeoff and landing—and without warning. Passengers aboard a Pan Am 747, which was taxiing in preparation for takeoff, had no warning when a KLM 747 just taking off plowed into the Pan Am jet in light rain and fog at Tenerife Airport on March 27, 1977. All 248 aboard the KLM flight perished, whereas 335 on board the Pan Am flight died and 61 survived. This accident remains the worst aviation disaster in history.

Nor did passengers or flight attendants aboard an otherwise uneventful National Airlines flight 193, making an instrument-landing approach to Pensacola Regional Airport at 9:20 P.M. on May 8, 1978, have even a moment's warning that the plane would crash into Escambia Bay. Fifty-five passengers and crew escaped the sinking plane and were rescued by a nearby tugboat and barge. Three passengers who had apparently escaped the plane nevertheless drowned—*perhaps because of erroneous assumptions*. At least 24 passengers and even the crew *assumed* the seat cushions were flotation devices. They were not. Life vests with emergency lights to aid night rescue were located beneath the seats the passengers had just fled.

Finally, make a rough head count of seated passengers to determine where the biggest crowd will be in an evacuation. If you have a choice between two equally safe and accessible exits, one with a mob trying to push through it and one with only a few passengers near it, the uncrowded exit should allow you quicker access to safety.

8. Buy Your Baby a Ticket and a Safety Seat

The safest way for your baby to fly is seat-belted in an automobile/airline safety seat. If your infant is not in one of these seats and the plane is headed for a crash, flight attendants will tell you to put your child on the floor like a piece of baggage, and one of the most vulnerable and most important people in your life will have absolutely no protection. That's what happened before the crash of United flight 232 in Sioux City; one infant died, while two others survived.

Even if there is no crash, a baby riding in your lap can fly out of your arms and suffer injuries in a hard landing or turbulence.

And, of course, whether in an airplane or automobile, *never* strap yourself and your baby into the same seat belt; in an impact, the infant would be crushed between your forward-moving body and the stationary seat belt.

If you own an automobile infant safety seat—and you should—it will do double-duty as an airline infant safety seat if the model is certified by the FAA. Because the safety seat needs its own aircraft seat to secure it to the plane, you'll have to buy your infant a ticket. If you haven't purchased a ticket for your baby, many airlines will leave a seat open next to yours to accommodate the safety seat; but if the flight is booked solid, you—and your baby—are out of luck.

Don't let the airline tell you such a seat is disallowed. "The FAA approves any car seat manufactured after 1985 that lives up to auto safety standards," says Matt Finucane, director of Air Safety and Health Issues for the AFA. "But the

seat *does* have to bear evidence of FAA approval."
(You'll find that on a fine-print label attached to
the seat.)

To avoid hassles, Finucane suggests you call
two different people at the airline to confirm
that the seat you want to use is acceptable.

In 1989, the FAA proposed a regulation that
would recommend but not mandate infant seats.
But in a strange twist, the deregulated demanded
greater regulation. The Air Transport Association, an airline industry trade association, asked
the FAA to *require parents* to put infants in safety
seats. The industry's request will likely prevail
when the FAA issues a rule expected in 1991.
"If we buckle up our child at 55 miles per hour,
why not at 550 miles per hour?" says Robert
Aaronson, ATA president.

Beneficial as it is, the ATA move is public
relations grandstanding. The airline industry
doesn't need a rule to better protect passengers;
nothing bars an airline from establishing a policy
requiring that infants be buckled into a safety
seat. So then what's the gimmick here?

The issue surrounding child seats has always
been a dollars-and-cents one: "Who pays for the
portable infant seat itself, and, if you need a
regular seat to buckle the infant seat into, who
buys the ticket for *that?*"

Consumer groups have lobbied to have the airlines buy the seats and make them available to
ticketed infants, the same way they provide chairs
that fare-paying adults sit in. The FAA proposal
requires the airlines to pay nothing. The ATA

proposal also requires that the airlines pay nothing. Instead, *parents* would have to buy the seats and the tickets.

That thinking is only partially correct. Parents *should not* balk at buying the infant seats, because they are already obligated by state laws to purchase such safety equipment for use in automobiles. That equipment is efficiently and easily transported onto an airplane. And if their child takes up space on a plane that could have been sold to someone else, they *should* buy a ticket.

Passengers with children and infants are a growing market segment for the airlines, however, and that means these customers are gaining clout. Use it. When making reservations, such passengers should speak to a ticketing supervisor and insist that the airline strike a deal—infant discount tickets (since an infant and seat add significantly less weight to the payload than a 150-pound adult with three pieces of luggage) or a nominal additional charge if empty seats are available and wouldn't have been sold. If you have no success there, study Chapter 7, then press your case with the airline's top brass. Sooner or later, the airlines will yield, if concerned consumers push hard enough.

9. Employ Precrash Planning

Precrash planning when an accident is imminent is a relatively simple process, complicated primarily by its life-or-death consequences. Let's go back to that fictitious plane crash you were in at the beginning of Chapter 2 to see how you got out of it alive. Precrash planning between the time you received warning of trouble and impact played a key role.

First, you fastened your seat belt. We recommend that you wear your belt securely *throughout every flight,* not just on the takeoff and landing or in turbulence. There are numerous cases of unbelted passengers being injured in sudden turbulence. When the roof blew off the Aloha Airlines Boeing 737-200 flight 243 in April 1988, all passengers were apparently belted in and consequently were *not* sucked out of the plane during the rapid cabin decompression. The flight attendant who was swept out of the plane and killed was *standing* near seat row 5.

Back to *our* fictitious accident. You were in seat 23D toward the rear of the plane, where the odds of surviving initial impact are greatest. You found the red light of the rear emergency exit and imprinted on your mind the number of rows separating your row (call it row zero) from the exit: three rows. You kept repeating that number in case the red light wasn't there after impact; indeed all the lights went out on impact, meaning you had to count off the rows with your hand in the darkness. If the cabin had filled with smoke before you got out of your seat in search of an exit, visibility would have been reduced, perhaps to zero.

Survivors from Air Canada flight 797 know the value of memorizing the location of exits in relation to their seat. On June 2, 1983, a smoldering fire broke out in the rear lavatory of this DC-9-32. It took only 20 minutes from the time the fire was discovered for the flight crew to land the plane at Greater Cincinnati International Airport. But in that short time the fire intensified and the cabin filled with smoke. After the plane landed and the exits were thrown open, many of the survivors who had moved aft to reach the overwing exits found them because they had memorized the number of rows between their seats and the exits and therefore counted the rows by feeling the seat backs as they moved aft. Two passengers were found dead where they collapsed in the aisle at rows 14 and 16—possibly because in the smoky environment they missed the emergency exit located at row 13.

Floor-mounted aisle emergency lights on many planes today were installed because of this accident. In smoke, they're supposed to help you locate the emergency exit; however, you cannot depend on these lights because the electricity often goes out in a crash and safety devices can malfunction. Thus, you must still count seats as a backup.

Although you fixed your mind on the rear exit as your best escape route, you also checked to see where other exits were and mapped out alternative escape routes.

You then looked at your fellow passengers and put them in three categories: (1) those who would probably make it out on their own, (2) those who might need your help—*if* it is possible for you to help them, and (3) those who could hinder your escape. This was pure guesswork, of course, and postimpact, some of the people you designated as Category 1's became Category 3's, whereas some Category 2's became Category 1's. The people remaining in Category 1 after impact took care of themselves.

You said to yourself that some in Category 2—handicapped persons, the elderly, children, and those lethally injured or trapped in the crash—should be assisted as much as possible, with regard to postimpact conditions. But you knew a rational and dispassionate calculation would have to be made: a 120-pound woman, for example, wouldn't be able to help that 250-pound man in seat 23A, *and you could endanger other survivors by helping him only enough to block an escape route;* the 60-pound child flying alone and sitting next to you in seat 23E was another story. You understood that even heroes can't save *everyone.*

Then the flight attendant said, "Passengers with babies, please place your infant on the floor between your feet. Do not belt the baby into your seat with you and do not attempt to hold the child in your arms." Neither in-lap baby in seat 15A and 19D was secured in an automobile/airline safety seat. The one in 15A died of impact trauma; the one in 19D somehow survived.

People in the third category could reduce your chances of survival, and in our accident, that included the woman in seat 22C who was becoming hysterical, the man in seat 26C who was clutching a briefcase full of important papers he didn't intend to leave behind, the man in seat 24E who had been a loud drunk for the previous 45 minutes of the flight, that heavyset man in seat 23A whose poor physical condition and weight worked against his survival, and even the 19-year-old in seat 20F who seemed to be a bit irresponsible.

With any one of these people on the escape route, your chances of survival would have been reduced.

Passengers with serious and debilitating physical impairments, unfortunately, also fall into this category, which is why federal regulations prohibit the seating of handicapped (or other passengers needing assistance) in exit and emergency exit rows, which must be kept clear.

The flight attendant then told passengers to "Please remove your shoes so as not to damage the inflatable escape chutes."

This put you in a quandary. You did not want to disobey safety instructions or endanger the lives of others by keeping your shoes on. But you were aware that after impact, walking barefooted through sheared metal shards, searing hot surfaces, puddles of burning fuel, broken glass, and other debris from the wreckage would have been perilous. We can't advise what to do about this. Women, however, should definitely remove high heels; always fly wearing flats.

Next, you guessed broadly at what kind of terrain you would most likely be crashing into. Because this flight has taken you over land, chances are you would crash on the ground. But you made mental provisions for the possibility of landing in a river, lake, or coastal waters. Under cold or stormy weather conditions, escape to water could greatly reduce your chances of survival. If you were over remote wooded areas, crashing into trees and uneven terrain could puncture the fuselage and possibly cause breakup of the craft into sections.

That means rows 12 through 20 might not be there after impact, and your best escape might be forward through the gaping hole rather than rearward through a potentially blocked exit door. An airport crash would mean that fire trucks, rescue personnel, and paramedics would be able to assist your survival efforts quicker. The point of this exercise was to prepare yourself for what crash-scene conditions you might have faced.

Finally, you checked again that your seat belt was secure, assumed the brace position—head between your knees, hands holding your ankles—and convinced yourself that you were going to be a survivor.

10. Carry a Simple Crash Survival Kit

Based on our analysis of the last two decades' airline accidents and in consultation with the Association of Flight Attendants and other experts, we've developed a crash survival kit that could save your life. Since the chances are excellent that you will *never* need this kit, we've kept it simple and inexpensive; no cumbersome parachutes, costly metal-cutting saws, or heavy fire extinguishers. You probably already own most of the items in the kit.

But an important reminder: While this kit could save your life, Ed Arbon of the Flight Safety Institute cautions, "The most important thing for you to do after impact is to start moving toward the exit." If your survival kit becomes misplaced, don't waste precious seconds looking for it. The kit is expendable; you are not.

The Ready for Take-off Crash Survival Kit contains:

1. *A durable, regular-size flashlight.* Emergency and cabin lighting frequently goes out after impact. A good flashlight will help you find your way. We prefer a standard-size light, as opposed to a bulky flashlight or too-dim penlight. *Matches or cigarette lighters are not an acceptable substitute because of the possible presence of unignited jet fuel and fumes at the crash site.*

2. *A Tupperware container or Ziploc plastic bag containing a wet (not just damp) facecloth or cloth hand towel.* Survivors of smoke-filled Air Canada flight 797, which had a fire smoldering in the rear lavatory in-flight, breathed through wet towels given to them by the flight attendants. The water in the wet towels actually filtered out much of the poisonous fumes (acid gases and hydrogen cyanide) and smoke—but *not* carbon monoxide. Dry clothing, napkins, or towels would not have been as effective.

A smoke hood—a plastic bag with an air filter attached to it—is a more expensive alternative, but we don't recommend it. We don't like the idea of covering the head in plastic during an emergency escape. Despite the hood's high-heat resistance to melting, the intense heat of an aircraft fire could exceed the upper-temperature tolerance of the plastic. The FAA has also determined that passengers are at risk of injuring themselves from improper use of a smoke hood.

3. *Durable-soled commuter's sneakers.* Women cannot easily escape an airline crash in high heels. Men's dress shoes can lose traction on wet or smooth, tilted surfaces. The best shoes have flat

sturdy soles, provide solid traction, stay on the foot, and are comfortable and stylish enough to wear throughout your flight. "Sneakers are a good idea," says Arbon. "They won't slip and won't puncture inflatable escape chutes and rafts."

4. *A bright red or white shirt or blouse.* In the event you're thrown from the plane (as many survivors are) and you are unconscious, brightly colored clothing that catches the eye of search and rescue teams could help you get medical attention quicker than if your colors camouflaged your body in the brush or wreckage.

5. *A lightweight fabric bag.* This is to carry your flashlight, and wet towel. The bag should be accessible from your seat and have a detachable strap that will secure it fast to your seat during impact without entangling your legs or arms—or anyone else's. Be sure to secure the bag tightly so that it does not slingshot around and injure you during impact.

11. Use Your Head in a Crisis

Once you realize you've survived impact, you've got to use your head and keep your wits. Hysterical passengers may shout orders to you that may or may not be trustworthy and of benefit to you: "Go to the front, the rear is about to explode!" "This door is stuck!" "Please, get my handbag for me!"

Listen to the flight attendants. They are trained and tested for emergency and crash situations.

Your body may work against you. Your mind may be racing and your senses may be hypersensitive. Don't let your biological red alert kill you by panicking. Some shocked passengers remain dumbly seated and awaiting instructions after impact unless a flight attendant tells them to get up and move.

Your key to survival after impact is to find the quickest, safest route out of and away from the plane. In some cases, survival may mean choosing a route that will almost certainly injure you. Some survivors have opened doors and punched their way through a wall of fire to escape—injured, but *with* their life.

Never forget that some *perceived* escape routes may really be dead ends, like the jammed rear exit doors on Delta flight 1141. Whenever you make a move, be aware of alternative routes and try to keep your options open as much as possible. At the same time, be ready to make decisions; a desire to keep too many options open could leave you indecisive, confused, and unable to move toward safety.

Finally, if the worst does happen and your plane goes down, fix your mind on this fact: you *can* survive.

CHAPTER 4

How to Find the Best Fare Deals

When United Airlines flight 105 departed Chicago for the west coast on July 1, every passenger had a similar experience. Everyone aboard the same roomy DC-10 left O'Hare Airport at the same time—8:25 A.M. CDT—and arrived as one at Los Angeles International Airport 4 hours and 5 minutes later at 10:30 A.M. PDT. Everyone enjoyed the nonstop aspect of the flight, almost everyone had the in-flight breakfast. Just about everyone's luggage went to the exact same baggage carousel.

But when it came to an area of vital concern to all passengers—airfares—the carbon-copy flight experience cost different passengers vastly different ticket prices. Passengers traveling first class, of course, paid the most—$833 one way— for the added legroom, better cabin service, and other first-class amenities. Coach passengers, however, paid one of seven different fares—ranging from as high as $557 one way to as low as $162.50 each way. Some passengers, using cost-cutting methods we'll explain shortly, may have paid even less.

The wide range of fares charged on flight 105 is not unusual. Just about every flight today has a similar pricing structure. And because airfares are a high priority for travelers, today's arcane pricing system has become a controversial subject.

But as with any emotionally charged issue, a large number of myths and misleading facts have sprung up, leading consumers to believe they are being gouged by the airlines. Consumer groups and members of Congress have charged that airline fares are higher today than they were before deregulation. Even trustworthy *Consumer Reports* magazine suggested that deregulation has cheated its readers with higher fares.

The effect of this onslaught of bad news in magazines, newspapers, and TV reports actually hurts consumers by creating the erroneous impression that there's nothing travelers can do to find good ticket prices. The "consumer-as-victim" slant also leads customers to believe they've been fleeced—even when they've gotten a bargain.

Are consumers being ripped off? Is the pricing system unfair? Is there even a shred of logic to today's confusing airfare setup? To find the answers, you have to separate the myths from the sometimes complex realities. Once you've eliminated all the confusing static surrounding the issue, you'll be better able to identify and grab the truly good airfare deals that *are* out there.

Myth: Airfares Have Skyrocketed

There is little evidence to support charges that airlines are mugging their customers. If airlines were truly price gouging, passengers—being rational consumers who don't have an unlimited supply of money but who *do* have other options—would fly less. They'd choose more cost-effective alternatives to air travel—a train or car instead of a plane for destinations within a few hundred miles; a teleconference instead of an in-person business meeting; or a motor vehicle vacation closer to home instead of air travel to a distant locale.

But consumers have *not* cut back their air travel. As Table 4-1 shows, airline passenger traffic is up 65 percent since 1978. More people fly today than ever before. In the last year alone, 51.5 million adults—29 percent of the adult population—took at least one plane trip.

Another expected outcome of airline profiteering would be profits—*big profits* running significantly higher than the 11 to 15 percent the companies could get investing in, say, the stock market. Yet here again the evidence is lacking. Table 4-2 shows that net airline industry profit margins have shrunk from 5.2 percent in 1978 to 0.3 percent in 1989. In the years between, margins fell even lower, to –2.5 percent in 1982, the year the industry lost $916 million.

From 1978 through 1989, the major airlines collected a total of $527 billion in revenues from customers. But after expenses and taxes, they were left with only $4.1 billion in profits. That

TABLE 4-1

Passenger Traffic at Major Airlines Is Up . . .

Year	Number of Passengers Boarded (millions)	Number of Flight Departures (millions)
1978	274.7	5.0
1979	316.7	5.4
1980	296.9	5.4
1981	286.0	5.2
1982	294.1	5.0
1983	318.6	5.0
1984	344.7	5.4
1985	382.0	5.8
1986	418.9	6.4
1987	447.7	6.6
1988	454.6	6.7
1989	453.7	6.6

Source: ATA.

TABLE 4-2

. . . While The Major Airlines' Profit Margins Are Down

Year	Net Profit Margin (%)	Total Revenues (millions)	Total Expenses (millions)	Net Profit After Taxes (millions)
1978	5.2%	$22,884	$21,519	$1.2
1979	1.3	27,227	27,028	0.3
1980	0.1	33,728	33,949	0.0
1981	–0.8	36,663	37,117	–0.3
1982	–2.5	36,408	37,141	–0.9
1983	–0.5	38,954	38,643	–0.2
1984	1.9	43,825	41,674	0.8
1985	1.8	46,664	45,238	0.9
1986	–0.5	50,525	49,202	–0.2
1987	1.0	56,986	54,517	0.6
1988	2.6	63,749	60,312	1.7
1989	0.3	69,340	67,475	0.2

Source: ATA.

works out to less than a 1 percent profit margin—not much different than the margin your local supermarket gets.

The average rate of return on what the airlines invested in the business from 1978 through 1989 was better, but still nothing to brag about; for every $1 the airlines invested to keep the planes flying, they earned just 7 cents in profit per year. That hardly qualifies as highway robbery, especially when critics of the airlines were probably earning an 8 to 9 percent return themselves if they held any of a number of standard personal investments—bank certificates of deposit, individual retirement accounts (IRAs), annuities, or stock mutual funds.

Other evidence shows deregulation has created bargains for consumers. A Brookings Institute study concluded that consumers were saving $5.7 billion a year in airfares thanks to deregulation, and a Federal Trade commission tally put the savings at $100 billion between 1978 and 1987. According to the Air Transport Association, 91 percent of the 454 million airline tickets sold in 1989 were discount fares, with prices slashed an average of 60 percent.

On average—and adjusted for inflation—today's airfares are 28 percent *lower* than they were before deregulation, according to industry and government statistics. Over the last decade, airfare increases, as measured by the amount of revenues collected per passenger mile flown, have generally *not* kept pace with increases in the Consumer Price Index (see Table 4-3). The General Accounting Office has also concluded that airfares have decreased on average and that by 1983 airlines "were charging fares lower than the level that would have been set by a [government regulated] fare formula used before [1978]."

TABLE 4-3

U.S. Scheduled Airline Fares Have Risen . . .
Until You Account for Inflation

Year	Average Revenue per Passenger Mile (cents)	Year-to-Year Change	Average Revenue per Passenger Mile Adjusted for Inflation (cents)	Year-to-Year Change
1978	8.3	−1.5%	8.3	−8.5%
1979	8.7	+4.9	7.8	−5.7
1980	11.0	+26.3	8.7	+11.3
1981	12.4	+12.4	8.9	+1.8
1982	11.8	−4.7	8.0	−10.2
1983	11.6	−1.1	7.6	−4.2
1984	12.1	+4.2	7.6	−0.1
1985	11.7	3.7	7.1	−7.0
1986	10.8	−7.5	6.4	−9.2
1987	11.1	+2.3	6.4	−1.3
1988	11.9	+7.5	6.6	+3.2
1989	12.4	+4.5	6.6	−0.3

Source: ATA.

Half-Truth: Airfares Have Risen

The effects of deregulation, of course, have not all been positive. A number of bad side effects have resulted, and it is those negatives that critics have overemphasized.

Chief among those that directly affect your pocketbook is that airfares on *some* routes *have* skyrocketed. The classic case study is the GAO's analysis of changes in airfares at St. Louis after TWA and Ozark Airlines merged in the fourth quarter of 1986. Before the merger, TWA was the dominant carrier, controlling 56 percent of the passenger boardings at St. Louis while Ozark was number two, with a 26 percent market share. No other airline had more than a 3 percent share. After the merger, TWA owned a sumo-wrestler-size 82 percent market share.

The GAO found that TWA's St. Louis fares on 67 nonstop routes increased 13 to 18 percent between the first three quarters of 1986 and 1987. At the same time, airfares nationally rose only 5 to 6 percent.

TWA responded to the findings by citing several factors that depressed its airfares in the base period—a flight attendants' strike and the Beirut hijacking of a TWA jet, which hurt traffic at the airline and forced the carrier to offer special discounts. The increases, TWA said, were not the result of its virtual market monopoly.

But another, larger GAO study showed that average airfare yields at 15 major airports dominated by just one or two airlines were 27 percent higher than the average yields paid at 38 other airports not dominated by any one carrier. The higher fares resulted from decreased competition. In some cases the decreased competition resulted from bigger airlines simply buying up the smaller competitors. At Minneapolis-St. Paul airport, for example, fares rose 25% after Northwest took over competitor Republic Airlines in 1986.

Dominant airlines at concentrated airports have also been able to squeeze out other carriers by monopolizing ownership of the limited number of airport gates. TWA, for example, holds long-term leases to roughly 75 percent of the available gates at Lambert-St. Louis International Airport, one of the concentrated airports studied by the GAO. In Pittsburgh, another concentrated airport in the GAO study, USAir has about 73 percent of the gates.

Deregulation has sparked airlines to attempt to control their markets in other ways. Computerized reservations systems (CRSs) owned by the airlines used to have biases built into their programs, which favored the CRS owner: the CRS owner's flights and fares appeared higher on display screens than the sometimes lower fares of competing airlines. In 1984, the now-defunct Civil Aeronautics Board prohibited such CRS bias, but a 1988 GAO study concluded that CRS owners still benefit from a number of anticompetitive features inherent in the setup.

Yet another dark cloud from deregulation is that regular unrestricted fares have risen dramatically. "Any traveler who needs flexibility of scheduling—and therefore must buy an unrestricted ticket—will generally pay two, three, or more times what he'd have paid under regulation," says Mel Brenner, a transportation consultant and former TWA and American Airlines vice president.

Lump it all together, and the bad-news side of deregulation presents consumers with a daunting and demoralizing picture. But as mentioned, that's only half the story—the worst half.

Fact: You Can Cut Your Airfares

For example, although unrestricted fares are significantly higher today than they were before deregulation, these so-called regular fares are more imaginary than real for most passengers. They are something like automobile sticker prices; most people don't pay them, they negotiate *down* from full-fare for a discount ticket. Because so many consumers—91 percent—accept the restrictions of a discount fare, presumably they're happy with the tradeoffs.

The bottom line is this: the fact that some airfares have gone through the roof is what gets all the media attention. The more significant and underreported story is that air travel today is cheaper than ever, and it can be made even cheaper by careful consumers who know how the airfare game is played.

How do you find a fare deal? Table 4-4 lists six major ways to cut your ticket prices. We've ranked them in order, starting with those that will give you the biggest break per hour of effort spent searching for and obtaining the deal. Ticket price-cutting methods toward the bottom of our ranking may not offer much bang for the buck, they may be associated with greater risk of low-quality services, or they may pertain only to special situations outside of your control.

TABLE 4-4

Seven Ways to Cut Your Airfare

Ranked best-to-worst in terms of estimated potential savings and effort required to find and capture the bargains.

Rank	Fare-cutting Technique	Estimated Potential Savings
1	Travel agent tour packages	30–80%
2	Advance purchase (APEX) tickets	40–70%
3	Smart shopping	40–60%
4	Special situation deals	5–70%
5	Travel agent assistance	5–40%
6	Ticket consolidators	10–30%

1. Travel Agent Tour Packages

Some of the best airfare deals by far can be found in tour packages offered by travel agencies, tour operators, and the package tour departments of the airlines themselves. Tour packagers are mum about exactly how low the airfare portion of your travel package costs: they bury the bargain air ticket within a bundle of other vacation-package elements—hotel, rental car, maybe even meals and entertainment. But the savings are huge.

"The lowest airfare in July from New York to Orlando was about $130 each way," says Steven Heydt, a senior vice president at New York's Liberty Travel, which claims to be the largest vacation-travel packager in the United States. "You'll pay far less than that if you buy a tour from us." For example, the same month, Liberty was offering four-day trips to Orlando that included round-trip airfare, hotel, and a rental car for as little as $558 per couple.

Heydt refuses to break down how much of that $558 goes to the hotel, how much to the car rental agency, and how much to the airline. But assume as much as half goes to the airline and the other half to the hotel and car rental agency. If that were the case, a couple would be paying just $280 for two round-trip tickets, or $70 each way. That's 46 percent off the lowest $130 fare and 75 percent off full fare.

How can travel agencies get such bargain fares for their customers? Essentially, tour package airfares are a way for airlines to unload unsold seats. On every flight an average 30 to 40 percent of the seats cannot be sold by the airline at even the lowest price. The seats would sell like hotcakes if the airline cut the price further, but if the airline did that, it would become increasingly difficult to maintain profitable fare levels on future flights. Consumers would eventually catch on and stop buying full- and discount-fare tickets until the fire-sale prices kicked in shortly before the departure date.

At the same time, airlines have a huge incentive to slash prices for these unsold seats, assuming the flight has reached the breakeven point where the number of seats sold covers the costs of the flight crew, fuel, maintenance, landing fees, overhead, and other items. Above breakeven, most of the revenue from every additional ticket sold goes right down to the bottom line— net income—because the incremental added cost of flying one more passenger is tiny. To get around the problem of undercutting its own prices, the airline quietly sells the tickets through the travel agent package tour.

2. Advance Purchase (APEX) Tickets

Another relatively easy way to cut your ticket costs significantly is to play ball with the airlines. Airlines will give you a discount if you barter with them. What can you give an airline? Three things are prized very highly:

1. A strong commitment that you'll show up at the airport in accordance with your reservations. Airlines ensure you'll do this when you make your reservations by giving you a discount in exchange for your forfeiting your right to a refund. Customers willing to agree to a 100 percent cancellation penalty—if you cancel your flight you get zero money back for your ticket—get the biggest breaks. Smaller penalties—50 percent, 25 percent—command smaller discounts.

2. Advance payment for your ticket. Again, the airline wants to line up passengers for as many seats as possible as far in advance of the departure date as feasible. Customers willing to buy their tickets 30 days in advance of departure get the biggest breaks. For shorter advance purchases—21, 14, 7, 3, 2 days—airlines give you a smaller discount.

3. Help in smoothing out traffic demand. If everyone flew when they wanted to, planes would be full of businesspeople flying to meetings on Mondays and returning on Fridays. Vacationers

would fill the planes on Saturdays. But midweek and Sunday the planes would be relatively empty. To smooth out the natural spikes in demand for air travel, the Saturday stayover was invented. If you stay at your destination on Saturday night, instead of flying back on Friday or Saturday, airlines will give you another discount. To get more pleasure travelers to fly midweek, APEX airfares from Tuesday through Thursday are reduced. Demand, of course, is also high at major holiday times—Christmas, Easter, Thanksgivings—because everyone who wants to fly has only a limited window of opportunity. Consequently, discounts are rarely available (blacked out, in ticket agent jargon) on peak demand dates. If you can juggle your holiday travel, however, you'll be more likely to find savings.

Most airline discounts and advertised limited-time "sale" prices are built around these concepts, and the idea is rather simple. Things, however, get more complex and the bargains lose some of their luster when the "Is the fare available?" question is asked by the customer. Availability is a factor of a back-office operations strategy called yield management.

In a nutshell, yield management is a sophisticated way to squeeze the highest yield (revenue) out of each passenger according to their travel needs and ability to pay. The airlines employ teams of yield management specialists and computers to accomplish what amounts to an "auction" of seats on every flight.

Starting with relatively predictable demand patterns for air travel, the actual cost of getting the flight in the air, and competition from other airlines, yield managers set up a grid of full fares and discount prices. Next, the airline estimates how many seats need to be sold at full fare and how many can be made available at the various discounts in order for the flight to be profitable.

The middle and final phases of yield management involve computerized monitoring of actual ticket sales for each flight day by day and even hour by hour. If the established mix of full-fare and discount tickets is not selling quickly enough (meaning customers think the price is too high), the computer program will make more discount tickets available. (Like program traders in the stock market, the airline's yield management computer program, in effect, issues a "sell" order. That depresses prices so more tickets can be sold.)

If, on the other hand, the discount tickets are selling like Popsicles in July, that sets off an alarm inside the microchips: prices are ridiculously low and the airline could get a higher price by simply demanding it. The computer then pulls the discount fares off the video display screens and tries to get full fare.

This monitoring and fine-tuning of the full-fare/discount mix goes on all day long. As a result, computers change discount fare availability more than 200,000 times *daily*. If you're an airline executive, stockholder of the company, economist, or accountant, yield management may be the greatest invention since the abacus. Consumers either love or hate yield management—depending on whether they get stuck paying full fare or reap a discount savings.

The trouble with yield management is that the airlines are robbing Peter (typically business travelers who can't make travel plans weeks ahead of time) to pay Paul (the pleasure traveler who *can* plan ahead). How do you stay on the right side of this computer logic?

If you're traveling for pleasure, make your plans as far in advance as possible, and be ready to adjust your travel to the airline's discount fare availability.

If you travel on business frequently, you may be wise to establish a relationship with one travel agent. If you bring all your business to one agent in one agency, he or she will likely give you good advice on timing your purchase. The more business you bring the agent, the more clout you have.

How can the agent help you? By looking at the computer reservations system to see how quickly a flight is filling up. From this information, your agent may be able to make an accurate prediction that sales are sluggish enough to prompt a release of more discount fares in the near future. Thus the agent may advise you to bide your time on the hunch that the discount fare that's not available today may become available tomorrow. Similarly, if today's bargains are moving fast, the agent may wisely counsel you to grab the discount fare now because tomorrow it will probably be gone.

Some agents also have pull with those airlines they do a lot of business with. Under some circumstances, they may be able to talk to a supervisor at the airline and ask that a "special accommodation" be made available for you. But you have to ask. Again, the longer-lasting your relationship and the more profitable business you bring the agent, the better your chances of getting special treatment.

Of course you don't *need* an agent. If you have to pay full fare three or four days before departure, make your own reservations. But then periodically call back the airline to ask about lower fares. Frequently, discount fares become available at the last minute. If a steal does become available, book that fare. Then, in a separate phone call, cancel your full-fare reservation. Since you were going to pay full fare, there should be no cancellation penalty, and because advance purchase was not required for the full fare, you haven't as yet laid out any money for the ticket.

A major drawback of APEX fares is an unexpected change in your travel plans. Seymour Sherman, president of Aircraft Parts Corp. in Farmingdale, NY, carries around a year-old $700 round-trip ticket from Los Angeles to Japan in his pocket. It's useless. Because of a death in his family, he had to change his plans. The airline wouldn't refund the no-refund fare.

If you think your plans could change, consider trip-cancellation insurance. Some policies won't reimburse you if you simply change your mind on a whim or if a business trip has become unnecessary. But policies typically cover you if you or a member of your traveling party becomes ill, is injured, dies, or is called to jury duty. Some policies pay out if you missed your flight because of an accident while you were en route to the airport.

But before you spend money on insurance, check the airline's cancellation policy. Carol and Frank Curran had nonrefundable tickets on Delta between Ft. Meyers, FL, and Newark. Carol became ill the day before departure. She provided Delta with a note from her doctor, and the airline refunded Carol's $200 ticket. If the ticket agent didn't inform you of the penalty, federal regulations void the penalty. But penalties are usually listed somewhere on your ticket, so you'd probably have a tough time winning this case in court.

You can, of course, raise hell with the airline. According to a source at Delta, customers call every day asking for refunds. To mitigate the wrath of customers, Delta and the other major airlines have changed some penalty rules. Now they allow passengers to change the continuing or return portion of a trip (but not the outbound flight) by paying a $75 fee, subject to certain conditions. In 1990, as Eastern Airlines' fortunes dove deeper into a tailspin, it was forced temporarily to adopt a non-cancellation-penalty policy on its APEX fares to counter passenger fears that they might lose their money if the bankrupt airline was liquidated.

We recommend going toe-to-toe with the airline. When we wanted to change the return time of a United restricted-fare ticket from San Francisco to New York, we were told there would be a 25 percent cancellation penalty—*and* that the new one-way return flight would cost more than the $567 round-trip ticket we held. We had not been told of these penalties for switching flight plans when we bought the tickets.

We talked to a supervisor and declared our intent to file a complaint with the USDOT if the matter were not satisfactorily resolved. We let her know we were aware of the rules, our rights, and the details of our contract of carriage with the airline. We were firm, and informed her that we would pursue this matter to our satisfaction, even if it meant taking the problem to United corporate headquarters in Chicago. We got the supervisor's name. We also got the change we wanted without penalty.

If you must change plans, don't throw in the towel. Negotiate! For more information about how to do so effectively, see Chapter 7.

3. Smart Shopping

Carefully shopping for a good airline fare can save you a fortune. Cruising the marketplace is particularly valuable when your options for APEX fares and travel agent tour packages have either run out or are not available.

To be a smart shopper, you've got to know the options available to you. At the same time, because shop-around savings tend to be smaller than the first two strategies we've already covered, you don't want to spend an inordinate amount of time hunting for a $30 per ticket savings.

One major timesaver is available to anyone with a personal computer and telephone modem. By subscribing to the Official Airline Guide Electronic Edition Travel Service (OAG), consumers can plug into a computer data base containing information about millions of flights for more than 600 airlines throughout the world. When you key in your travel dates, departure airport, and destination, the OAG spews out lists of all fares and schedules offered by the airlines flying the route—*with lowest fares shown first.*

Computerization, of course, allows you great versatility in your hunt for the best travel plans. By punching in the correct commands, you can direct the OAG to give you information about all airlines flying the route or only your favorites. You can exclude from your search airlines that have given you poor service in the past. Your search can cover all flights or eliminate connecting flights, leaving you with information only on direct flights. You can search for the best fare or the best schedule. As you zero in on the flight you want, OAG will tell you if seats are available for the fare you want, what kind of aircraft you'll be flying, and the on-time performance record for that flight. In many cases, you can even book your own reservations through the computer and Thomas Cook Travel U.S.A. The data base is updated with more than 40,000 changes daily.

There is a $25 initial hookup fee. Subscribers also pay 47 cents for each minute they're connected to the OAG during prime time (Monday through Friday, 8 A.M. to 6 P.M. Central Time). The service is much less expensive to use during off-peak hours—just 17 cents a minute (your telephone company, of course, also charges you for your phone time). The cost of having all this information at your fingertips is a consideration, but even if you spend an hour searching for the best deal, you should be able to find savings that more than pay for the $10.20 worth of off-peak computer time.

Computer novices and those unfamiliar with the OAG data base may find the search process somewhat time-consuming. But the more you use the system, the more proficient you'll become at it and the simpler your searches become. The system does have time-saving shortcuts, including an "expert" mode that eliminates repetitive command explanations. OAG will also give you a free training session if you need it.

The OAG Electronic Edition Travel Service also provides an abundance of other travel data— arrival, departure, and gate information for 14 major airports; information and room rates on more than 37,500 hotels worldwide; weather reports; U.S. State Department Travel Advisories; news from *OAG Frequent Flyer* magazine and *Travel Management Daily News;* ski reports; quality ratings of hotels, motels, and restaurants in 145 U.S. cities; information on tours, discount travel, and cruises; currency rates; information on resort condominiums; and much more. For the frequent traveler, the OAG Electronic Edition is an invaluable service. Throughout this book, we encourage you to gather information such as on-time performance, fares, and type of aircraft used. The OAG is one way to find the up-to-the-minute data you're looking for.

No computer? Then use the telephone and the airlines' toll-free 800 numbers to shop for the best fare. Dealing with telephone ticket agents, however, is a lot like playing 20 questions: the agent has computer access to *all* the information and will be glad to tell you everything you want to know, but you must know how to coax the information out of him or her.

Actually, telephone shopping is a computer search through a middleman. You ask the ticket agent for information, the ticket agent asks the computer, the computer spits out data, and the ticket agent repeats what the computer shows.

Understand the process, though. As with a computer search, you start out with a broad request for information, then, with each choice you make, the search narrows. Some kind of answer will be found at the end of the search path, but it may not be the answer you're looking for; for example, you may be told that no discount fare is available for that date. What do you do then? Don't just accept the answer as pertaining to *all* flights on *all* dates from *all* airports. You've got to backtrack and try a different path. What about departing three days later? What if I took a flight at a different time of day? Could I get a better fare by flying from or to a different airport? How about a connecting flight instead of a direct one?

It can be a time-consuming process. Don't be intimidated by that fact, and don't make a reservation just because you don't want to ask the ticket agent to make a sixth data search for you. The agent is trying to get your business for the airline: if he or she has to stay on the phone with you for a half-hour or an hour because of the airlines' complex fare structure, that's just the cost of doing business. (If, however, you feel uncomfortable about taking up so much of the ticket agent's time, thank the agent for the help, hang up, and redial the 800 number. You can then pick up where you left off with a different agent.)

To make sense of either your telephone shopping or your OAG search and to keep track of all the confusing fare and schedule possibilities, use the Ready for Take-off Travel Planner, Worksheet 4-1. The worksheet will also help you organize your search.

WORKSHEET 4-1

The Ready for Take-off Travel Planner

I. Ultimate destination: _____

II. Travel Date Calendar Grid (Fill in the dates in sequence
from earliest possible departure
to latest possible return.)

Month(s): _____

	Sun	Mon	Tue	Wed	Thu	Fri	Sat
Earliest travel dates	___	___	___	___	___	___	___
	___	___	___	___	___	___	___
Preferred travel dates	___	___	___	___	___	___	___
	___	___	___	___	___	___	___
Latest travel dates	___	___	___	___	___	___	___
	___	___	___	___	___	___	___

continued

III. Airlines to Consider

(First Choice to Last)	Phone number
1 _____	1-800-_____
2 _____	1-800-_____
3 _____	1-800-_____
4 _____	1-800-_____
5 _____	1-800-_____

IV. Alternate Airports (Include estimated amount of time to drive from home and destination to the nearby airports.)

Near Home	Drive Time	Near Destination	Drive Time
1 _____	_____	1 _____	_____
2 _____	_____	2 _____	_____
3 _____	_____	3 _____	_____
4 _____	_____	4 _____	_____

V. Fare and schedule options (CNXT = A connecting flight; note that departure and arrival times are local time.)

1111 Airline flight #	Airport	Date	Depart Time	Arrive Time	Fare and Restrictions
Originating Flight(s)					
CNXT					
CNXT					
Return Flight(s)					
CNXT					
CNXT					

continued

2222 Airline flight #	Airport	Date	Depart Time	Arrive Time	Fare and Restrictions

Originating Flight(s)

CNXT
CNXT

Return Flight(s)

CNXT
CNXT

3333 Airline flight #	Airport	Date	Depart Time	Arrive Time	Fare and Restrictions

Originating Flight(s)

CNXT
CNXT

Return Flight(s)

CNXT
CNXT

4444 Airline flight #	Airport	Date	Depart Time	Arrive Time	Fare and Restrictions

Originating Flight(s)

CNXT
CNXT

Return Flight(s)

CNXT
CNXT

Here's how to shop either by phone or computer using the travel planner:

I. List your ultimate destination. For example, "Los Angeles," or "Southern California," or simply "California." The bigger your target, the greater your airport, fare, and schedule options.

II. Fill in all the possible dates on which you may be able to travel. If you're planning a two-week vacation sometime in October or November 1991, start with your earliest possible departure date, say October 10, which falls on a Thursday. On Thursday of the first line ("Earliest travel dates"), write "10." Then, in proper sequence, fill in the remaining dates in October and November until you reach the absolute last possible day of travel that marks the end of your vacation.

This travel date calendar grid includes your preferred vacation time, but also shows how flexible your travel plans can be. This grid will be an important ready reference when the ticket agent proposes alternate travel dates on which discount fares are available.

III. Based on which airline provides the best quality service you're looking for (see Chapters 5 and 6), your past good and bad experiences with the various airlines, and any other factors you deem important, list the airlines you would consider using for your travel. Start with the most preferred airline—whether it's your favorite because of high-quality service or low price.

Which airlines charge the least? You won't know that for a given flight and time until you gather the data yourself. On average, however, some airlines tend to charge less than others. We analyzed fare data from members of the Air Transport Association (ATA), which tend to be larger carriers. Each airline's total passenger revenue for 1989 was divided by the total number of revenue passenger miles the airline flew. The result is the average fare charged per revenue passenger mile, measured in cents. This is the basis for our rating, with the lower average fares appearing highest in the ranking. We then multiplied that number by 1,908 miles—which was the length of the average round-trip flight in 1989—to show what the average trip ticket would cost.

Table 4-5 ostensibly shows which airlines on average charge passengers the least and which charge the most. But because every route is different, don't just assume that if lower-ranked USAir and higher-ranked TWA are competing for passengers on the same route, TWA's fare will be lower and that you need not call USAir to find out what it is charging. TWA may be cheaper, USAir may be cheaper, or both may charge exactly the same amount. The only way to determine which one charges less on a specific route is to call up and ask about fares on that route.

What Table 4-5 actually shows is the true corporate attitude toward pricing, despite whatever the airline's advertisements might claim. Which airline is more likely to strike a price bargain with customers to get their business? Low-priced airlines like Hawaiian, Pan Am, and Southwest are serious about deal making. If you're interested in a good price, these airlines are where

TABLE 4-5

Who Will Strike a Fare Deal with Passengers?

Ranked most-likely to least-likely to bargain for your business based on the *unrounded* average fare per revenue passenger mile in 1989. Average fares shown here have been rounded to the nearest cent.

Rank	Airline	Average Fare Per Revenue Passenger Mile	Charge for Average Length Roundtrip (1,908 miles)
1	Hawaiian Airlines	$0.09	$175.54
2	Pan Am	0.10	194.62
3	Southwest Airlines	0.10	198.43
4	TWA	0.11	207.97
5	Continental	0.11	211.79
6	Eastern*	0.12	223.24
7	American	0.12	228.96
8	United	0.12	230.87
9	Northwest	0.12	234.68
10	Midway Airlines	0.12	240.41
11	Canadian Airlines	0.13	255.67
12	Delta	0.14	257.58
13	USAir	0.16	301.46
14	Alaska Airlines	0.17	328.18
15	Air Canada	0.18	339.62
16	Aloha Airlines	0.23	438.84
17	American Trans Air	0.50	959.72

Source: Ready for Take-off Database, ATA.

* In bankruptcy.

The information contained in this table is updated regularly in *Ready for Take-off Database,* a quarterly publication. For subscription information, write to: *Ready for Take-off Database,* P.O. Box 521, Easton, PA 18044-0521.

you should *start* looking. High-priced airlines, like American Trans Air Aloha, USAir, Air Canada, and Alaska Airlines, on the other hand, are more tightfisted.

But every assessment of an airline's prices must factor in the quality of service. (Chapters 5 and 6 will help you assess airline service quality.) Customer surveys give American and United generally high marks for service. Considering those airlines' lower to mid-range prices, their exceptional service is actually a bargain.

USAir, conversely, is not known for giving customers the red-carpet treatment, yet passengers pay regal prices to fly this carrier. Management may point to the somewhat higher costs associated with the short-haul flights that are at the heart of USAir service. But Hawaiian and Southwest are short-hop airlines too; how do *they* have significantly better prices than USAir, and better fares than some of the long-haul majors?

IV. Find the two or three airports within a reasonable driving distance from your home. Next, find two to four airports you might use in the vicinity of your destination. List these on your travel planner.

Creatures of habit, many air travelers are comfortable with the familiar surroundings of their nearest airport, and will always fly out of there. On the destination side, they know they need to travel to business on, say, the outskirts of Cleveland, and they *assume* there's only one place to get off the plane there—Cleveland-Hopkins International Airport, coded "CLE" on the ticket.

Both assumptions are short-sighted. Flyers to-day often have a choice of two or three airports, and the options are increasing as airlines try to find relief from packed-to-capacity major airports by expanding service at smaller surrounding fields. Washingtonians, for example, can choose from three major airports: Washington National, Dulles International, and Baltimore-Washington International. Los Angelenos have their pick of *seven*: Los Angeles International, of course, plus Long Beach Municipal Airport, Burbank-Glendale-Pasadena Airport, Ontario International, John Wayne Airport in Orange County, and at the north and southeast extremes of the metropolitan area, Santa Barbara Municipal Airport and Palm Springs Regional.

Finding a selection of airports may be easier at your destination. For example, if you're vacationing in Florida, your plans may include rental-car travel to two or three sections of the state. Say you plan to spend two weeks at Daytona Beach and will also visit Disney World (in Orlando) and Busch Gardens (in Tampa). You can "enter" the state at any one of four decent-sized airports: Melbourne Regional or Daytona Beach Regional on the Atlantic coast; Orlando International; or Tampa International.

What's the difference? One airport may have flights from your city landing several times throughout the day. Another airport may be served by your favorite airline. A third may simply offer a more pleasant experience from gate to baggage claim to the airport exit. The most compelling reason for the purposes of this chapter is to find a cheaper fare. Let's examine the Florida vacation to see how choice of airport can affect prices for a family of five.

Assume the family lives in Fort Atkinson, WI, about 40 miles from Madison's Dane County Regional Airport, which is the airport they usually use. They've determined that they'll fly to their beachfront hotel in Daytona Beach on October 1 and return October 14. During the vacation, they'll drive to Orlando to see Disney World and Tampa to see Busch Gardens. Like most families, they're interested in cutting their airfare, because with five tickets to buy, every dollar saved on the ticket is multiplied by five. They make reservations and buy restricted APEX tickets from American Airlines to keep costs down. The best round-trip fare from Madison to Daytona (via connecting flight): $373 apiece or $1,865 for the family. That's actually a good deal, because the full unrestricted fare would have cost $1,092 per round-trip, a whopping $5,460 for the whole brood. The APEX fares saved them 66 percent.

But they could save even more by exploring the airport option. By flying Madison to Tampa, they would pay only $288 apiece round-trip, the best fare available on that route. By rearranging their schedule somewhat to put the Busch Gardens visit at either the beginning or end of their trip, the 136-mile drive from Tampa to Daytona Beach would add no more mileage to their vacation, because they were planning to make the Daytona-Tampa trek anyway.

Now look at what they could save by flying Midwest Express from Madison to Orlando. The best round-trip APEX fare: $274. Total cost for five tickets: $1,370. That's $818 less than the "best deal" between Madison and Daytona Beach and 75 percent off the full fare between those points.

The family from Fort Atkinson has other airport options near home—Chicago's O'Hare International (85 miles southeast) and Midway Airport (100 miles southeast), General Mitchell International Airport in Milwaukee (45 miles east), and Greater Rockford Airport in Rockford, IL (55 miles south). Table 4-6 shows the lowest unrestricted and APEX round-trip airfares between these and Madison's airports and the four possible Florida destinations considered earlier.

TABLE 4-6

What a Difference an Airport Makes

Lowest Airfares Available Between Nine Airports
(Unrestricted Roundtrip, October 1991)

Airport (code)	Daytona Beach, FL (DAB)	Melbourne, FL (MLB)	Orlando, FL (MCO)	Tampa, FL (TPA)
Madison (MSN)	$1092	$1092	$832	$842
Milwaukee (MKE)	702	794	702	720
Chicago O'Hare (ORD)	464	454	720	668
Chicago Midway (MDW)	902	NO SERVICE	720	744

continued

| Rockford (RFD) | 902 | 782 | 804 | 818 |

| | Lowest Airfares Available Between Nine Airports (APEX Roundtrip, October 1991) | | | |

Airport (code)	Daytona Beach, FL (DAB)	Melbourne, FL (MLB)	Orlando, FL (MCO)	Tampa, FL (TPA)
Madison (MSN)	$373	$373	$274	$288
Milwaukee (MKE)	226	226	226	227
Chicago O'Hare (ORD)	220	220	221	221
Chicago Midway (MDW)	228	NO SERVICE	300	300
Rockford (RFD)	265	278	268	268

Source: *Ready for Take-Off*, OAG

As you can see from the fare grid, shopping for the best airport combination can save you significant amounts. The difference between highest and lowest "best" APEX fares among the 20 city-pair combinations was $153, or a 41 percent potential savings. For unrestricted full fares, the dollar difference between the highest and lowest "best" fare was greater—$638—a 58 percent savings. These savings are worth hunting for, especially if you have to travel on a moment's notice and your advance purchase saving options have already run out.

Why is one route cheaper than another? Consumer demand for airline seats between the two points is one reason. If only 50 people a day want to fly from Point A to Point B, it's risky enough for one airline to operate one 60-seat jet on the route; riskier still is for a new competitor to put a second 60-seater in service between the same two points. With 120 seats battling for the same 50 customers, losses are guaranteed, and unless the established carrier is wildly price-gouging, it will be tougher for the new airline on the block to draw customers than it is for the old familiar carrier to retain its customer base. There's simply not enough business to fight over. Big customer demand routes—New York/Chicago, Los Angeles/Honolulu, Dallas-Ft. Worth/Houston— tend to have lower prices than less popular routes.

The amount of competition on the route is another reason. American's smallest Madison-Melbourne fare is $373, whereas its best Chicago-Melbourne fare is only $278 because American has less competition between Madison and Melbourne. On the Chicago-Melbourne route, however, American has to compete with Delta, USAir, and Eastern. To attract customers and stay in business, all four airlines have to keep their prices as low as possible (or offer some compelling reason for a higher price, such as better-quality service).

BOX 4-1

How Good Is Your Airport?
—Airfares—

We explained earlier that airfares at so-called concentrated airports, where competition was stifled, tend to be higher than at unconcentrated airports where healthier levels of competition exist. The GAO listed the 15 concentrated airports in its study where fares were an average 27 percent higher than at unconcentrated airports. Table 4-7 lists these airports. The listing also shows the dominant carriers and how much greater their fare yields were than average fares at the more competitive airports as of the fourth quarter of 1988. The airports are ranked worst to less-worse based on how much higher their dominant carriers' airfares are above average fares at competitive airports.

You can complain about these airlines taking advantage of the downtrodden consumer by writing your congressional representative about the problem. But if you really want to accomplish something, the most effective way to put the airlines back in their place and protect yourself from a fleecing is to use your consumer power of the purse and avoid buying tickets from the dominant carriers at these airports—if you can.

For example, instead of flying Delta out of Atlanta, where it charges an average 80 percent above what airlines at more competitive airports charge, explore other carriers flying out of there—American, United, Northwest. You needn't make a point of this out of spite; you have a strong financial incentive. According to the GAO study, the airfares of most other airlines in Atlanta run about 30 percent lower than Delta's.

continued

You might also try avoiding the major airports altogether. Instead of using Greensboro-Douglas International, you could fly out of (or into) slightly less-exorbitant Raleigh-Durham. Possible alternatives to Greater Cincinnati Airport are Blue Grass Airport in Lexington, KY, Standiford Field in Louisville, KY, and Indianapolis International in Indiana.

TABLE 4-7

Skyway Robbery

Fifteen airports where reduced competition will cost you money, ranked Worst to Less-Worse, based on how much higher the dominant airlines' airfares were above average fares at competitive airports at the end of 1988. Equally bad percentages are arranged alphabetically by airport.

Airport	Dominant Airline	If Competitive Airport Airfares Equal 100%, this Is the Percent Dominant Airlines Charge Here
Charlotte-Douglas International	USAir	180%
Greensboro Regional	USAir	180%
Hartsfield Atlanta International	Delta Texas Air	180% 160%
Greater Cincinnati	Delta	153%
Memphis International	Northwest	153%
Nashville Metropolitan	American	150%

continued

Airport	Dominant Airline	If Competitive Airport Airfares Equal 100%, this Is the Percent Dominant Airlines Charge Here
Syracuse Hancock International	USAir	150%
Greater Pittsburgh International	USAir	147%
Raleigh-Durham	American	147%
Salt Lake City International	Delta	147%
Dayton International	USAir	140%
Detroit Metropolitan	Northwest	120%
Minneapolis/St. Paul	Northwest	120%
Lambert-St. Louis	TWA	113%
Denver Stapleton International	Texas Air United	107% 107%

Source: GAO.

Data as of fourth quarter 1988.

4. Special Situation Deals

There are a number of other ways to get a break on a ticket. The savings can be small or large, but typically these savings apply only to certain flights, special situations, or certain qualified passengers.

Special discounts for the elderly. All the major airlines offer senior citizens an additional 10 percent discount off any fare. Thus, on its $230 round-trip APEX fare from Omaha to Atlanta, American Airlines, for example, would cut $23 off the price, reducing the fare to $207. In some cases, one nonsenior traveling with the elderly passenger can also get a 10 percent discount off his or her fare.

Eight airlines—American, Delta, Continental, Eastern, Northwest, TWA, USAir and United—offer seniors an alternative break as well—special multi-coupon booklets. As shown on Table 4-8, prices range from $379 to $472 for the 4-coupon booklets and from $640 to $792 for the 8-coupon books. Generally, each coupon is good for one-way passage to or from your destination in the United States (one way to Alaska and Hawaii, however, will cost you two coupons). Numerous restrictions apply, and you should contact each airline for details.

The value of these fixed-fare coupons varies. Obviously, the more expensive the full- and APEX-fare rates on a particular flight are, the more valuable your coupon. To determine whether you should use a coupon or a lowest fare available to the general public, calculate the per-ticket dollar cost of each coupon (divide the purchase price of the booklet by the number of tickets in the booklet) or refer to table 4-8.

This table shows that TWA offers the best senior coupon deal—a cost of just $95 per coupon for the 4-coupon book. But even the coupons that others charge $19 to $22 more apiece for are still a bargain worth pursuing. For our money, with prices this low and this close, we'd make

TABLE 4-8

Who Loves Grams Most?

Airline discounts for senior citizens, ranked in order of biggest to smallest potential savings. Equal-value deals are ranked alphabetically by airline.

Airline	Coupon Booklet Price 4-coupon 8-coupon	Fare Value per Coupon 4-coupon 8-coupon	Senior Citizen Discount (off any fare)
TWA	$379 NA	$95 NA	10%
Continental	$384 640	$96 80	10%
Northwest	$384 640	$96 80	10%
American	$420 704	$105 88	10%
United	$420 704	$105 88	10%
USAir	$420 704	$105 88	10%
Eastern	$428 720	$107 90	10%
Delta	$472 792	$118 99	10%
Pan Am	NA	NA	10%

Source: *Ready for Take-off Database*, airline data.

NA = Not Applicable.

The information contained in this table is updated regularly in *Ready for Take-off, Database* a quarterly publication. For subscription information, write to: *Ready for Take-off Database*, P.O. Box 521, Easton, PA 18044-0521.

the purchase based on the quality of these four airlines' service rather than on price. That would make high-quality American's, United's, and Delta's coupons a steal.

Special discounts for the bereaved. Your brother Max from Peoria just passed away and you have to fly on a moment's notice to his funeral. You think you'll have to take a bath on full-fare tickets, right?

Not necessarily. If you choose the right airline, you can save. Most major airlines offer some special bereavement or emergency discount fare (see Table 4-9). Pan Am and United are the insensitive exceptions.

TABLE 4-9

Which Airlines Have Sympathy?

Airline bereavement fares, ranked best to worst, based on Ready for Take-off's assessment of the estimated value of the discount. Roughly similar deals ranked alphabetically.

Airline	Bereavement Discount
Northwest	50 percent discount off full coach fare.
Delta	45 percent discount off full fare.
TWA	33% off full coach fare.
American	Varies; up to 35 percent off full fare
Continental	No set policy, Generally 35% off full fare.
USAir	7-day APEX fare with advance purchase and Saturday stayover requirements waived. Cancellation penalties do apply.
Eastern	3-day APEX fare with advance purchase and Saturday stayover requirements waived. Cancellation penalties do apply.

continued

Airline Bereavement Discount

United	No published discounts.
Pan Am	No discounts.

Source: *Ready for Take-Off,* airline information.

The information contained in this table is updated in *Ready for Take-off Database,* a quarterly publication. For subscription information, write to: *Ready for Take-off Database,* P.O. Box 521, Easton, PA 18044-0521.

Northwest and Delta offer the best deals—50 percent and 45 percent off full coach fare. American makes its bereavement deals on a case-by-case basis, according to sources at the airline, which suggests that poor negotiators may not get the top 35 percent discount.

These fares generally apply to the death of immediate family members—parents, children, siblings, and the step-family equivalents. For the death of an aunt, uncle, or fourth cousin, you'll have to pay full fare. In some cases, the fare is available if the person you're flying to is still alive but his or her death is imminent. (You won't qualify, however, if the family member you're rushing to visit has, say, six more months to live.) To prevent phony death claims, the airlines require varying measures of proof—death certificate, copy of a newspaper obituary mentioning your relationship to the deceased, or the phone number of the funeral home where the deceased will be laid out.

Fly by night. In some cases, late-night to early-morning flights (like the red-eye flights from the

West Coast) are slightly cheaper than flights at more traditional hours. USAir's through-the-night flight from San Francisco to New York costs $439 one way versus $477 for the one-way unrestricted fare—a $38 savings whose value only *you* can determine.

Exploit quirks in the pricing system. Because air travel prices are not just based on distance between two points but involve other factors like competition and efficiency, a number of airfare anomalies can be found in the pricing system—if you look hard enough.

What kind of oddities? The "hidden-city fare" is one. Suppose it's July 4 and you suddenly have to fly from Salt Lake City to New York the next day. On such short notice, the best fare—on Pan Am—is $301 each way. If only you were flying from Salt Lake City to Washington, DC; Pan Am only charges $208 each way for that flight.

As it turns out, Pan Am's flight from Salt Lake City to Washington National Airport isn't a direct flight, it's a connecting flight through ... JFK Airport in New York. By booking the Salt Lake City to Washington flight one way, you can get off the plane in New York and save $93. Obviously, you shouldn't check any baggage, because it will continue on to Washington. And you'll have to pay the full $301 fare back to Salt Lake City from New York in a separate ticketing transaction, but the savings may be worth it.

The airlines argue that booking your flights like this is against the rules and they're working to eliminate such hidden savings. On top of that, hidden-city bargains are tough to find, and the Salt Lake City-New York-Washington example is unusually generous as these savings go.

An even harder-to-find savings is the split-ticket maneuver. Say you want to fly from Dallas-Ft. Worth to Los Angeles. The best APEX fare for May 30 was $364 round-trip on Northwest. You could cut your fare by flying from Dallas to Albuquerque ($82 round-trip on Southwest Airlines) then from Albuquerque to Los Angeles ($92 round-trip on USAir). The total price of the split-ticket was $174—$190 less than the direct fare.

Such savings *are* out there, but they're so few and far between as to make them generally unworthy of your time spent searching. Some travel agents make it their business to find these oddities, and if your travel agent is so inclined, you might save a few bucks. But every search for air travel cost savings must also account for the value of the time spent finding the bargain. In this case, chances are good that the costs will outweigh the savings.

5. Travel Agent Assistance

Though no one absolutely *needs* a travel agent to find a low fare, having a trusted agent can help. Beyond travel agent tour packages and help timing your APEX purchase mentioned earlier, travel agents can save you money if they charge a set fee for their services rather than a commission. Typically, 10 percent of a ticket's price goes to the travel agent. That's $50 on a $500 fare.

If you travel frequently, fly first class, or bring the entire family; those 10 percent commissions can add up fast.

A fee-only agent will rebate that money to your wallet, minus a service fee. For example, the Travel Avenue agency in Chicago gives customers an 8 percent rebate off the base fare, then charges only an $8 fee per domestic trip and $20 per international trip. Thus, if the base fare is $300, Travel Avenue gives you a $24 rebate, then adds back an $8 fee. Net fare: $300 − $24 + $8 = $284. That's a 5 percent savings. If you've already done the legwork finding the best fare, why should you pay a commission to have an agent spend only two or three minutes punching some numbers into a computer reservations system keyboard and printing out the ticket?

To find a fee-only agent, you have to phone around town. Some advertise. Travel Avenue (formerly the McTravel Agency) operates nationwide and can be reached toll-free at 800-333-3335. But even a travel agency that usually works on commission may agree to a fee-only arrangement if you bring them enough business. "If I'm selling someone five or ten tickets, I'll charge a flat fee," admits one travel agent. Any business traveler, small-business owner, or pleasure traveler who brings an agent $2,000 to $3,000 or more per year in ticket sales is a big customer and should think about using his or her clout to get a fee-only arrangement, or at least a discount. Some 24 percent of those who have flown in the past 12 months took four or more trips, according to a survey by the Gallup Organization; 45 percent took only one trip.

If you're making flight arrangements for a large group, you can skip the agent altogether; the airline will be glad to *negotiate* the fare with you directly.

Whenever you deal with an agent on commission, beware of TACOs— Travel Agent Commission Overrides. If an agency steers a great many customers to airline X, boosting its sales volume above a certain threshold, the airline will often pay the agency more than the normal 10 percent commission. "TACOs go up to 12 to 15 percent commissions on *all* the agency's volume for the airline," explains Voit Gilmore, president of the American Society of Travel Agents.

So an agency that would earn $100,000 in commissions on $1 million in ticket sales for one carrier might earn proportionately more if it goes over the $1 million mark—commissions of, say, $143,000 on $1.1 million in sales versus only $110,000 without the TACO. That extra $33,000 provides a considerable incentive for the agent to get in the habit of finding the "best" ticket deals on the same airline, the airline that's quietly making the bonus $33,000 "payment."

If that sounds shady, travel agents can thank themselves: they imply a dirty deal's afoot by refusing to talk about the subject. "No comment!" snapped one agent at a major New York travel agency whom we asked about TACOs. "The fact that I get paid $1 or $1 million for my service is no one's business."

Nothing could be further from the truth. Because of the murky nature of the customer/travel agent/airline relationship, consumers need to know what money is changing hands both over *and* *under* the table. Many consumers assume travel agents are working for them, and travel agents keep this myth alive. But that's not how airlines see things; they believe the airline—not the customer—is the agent's boss. "The travel agent is the agent of the air carrier," says David Swierenga, spokesman for the ATA. Follow the money trail and you'll see Swierenga is correct. Although customer checks are written out to the travel agency, consumers are actually paying $500 to the airline for its services and the airline then pays its agent $50 for making the sale. Some 80 percent of all airline tickets are sold through travel agents, which makes them the airlines' de facto sales staff.

Though an agent may not put you on a higher-fare airline just because of a TACO, you have a right to know whether a potential conflict of interest exists. The only way to find out is to ask the agent which airlines are paying or have paid his or her agency TACOs. If you're booked onto one of those airlines, ask for the agent's assurance—and proof—that there are no better deals on competing airlines. Agencies that belong to the American Society of Travel Agents (ASTA) have a code of ethics that requires honest, straightforward dealings with the public. That, we believe, should include full disclosure about TACOs and commissions. Ask for a written breakdown of what you're paying the airline and what you're paying in agent commissions.

Some agents bridle when asked about TACOs, but if these bonuses are not influencing an agent's booking decisions, he or she has nothing to hide from you. If an agent refuses to discuss TACOs or commissions, refuse to give the agent your business. Consumers with complaints about travel agents can write to ASTA, Consumer Affairs Department, P.O. Box 23992, Washington, DC 20026.

Another incentive for an agent to show favoritism toward one airline is related to the computer reservation system (CRS) to which the agency is connected. Airlines own the CRSs (see Table 4-10) and offer them to travel agents to help them find the best flights. Travel agents pay subscription fees to use the CRSs, but these are subject to negotiation. Travel agencies, grateful to the CRS owner for the system hardware, service, training, and (perhaps) the negotiated price, may favor the CRS owner and book more flights on that airline, even though lower-fare options may exist.

Of course, the agent may not care which airline supplied the expensive computer hardware

TABLE 4-10

Who Helps Your Travel Agent Find You the "Best" Deal?
(Computerized Reservation System Owners)

CRS Name	Principal Owner	CRS Market Share
SABRE	American	37%
Apollo	United	32%
WORLDSPAN/PARS	TWA, Northwest, Delta	12%
System One	Continental Holdings	12%
DATAS II	Delta	5%

Source: WORLDSPAN, American, United.

and will use the CRS to find the best deal regardless of airline. To protect your flank, though, ask the agent which CRS he or she uses. As with TACOs, if the agent just happens to book you on the CRS owner's airline, ask for justification of the agent's choice and proof that a better deal is not available on another airline.

6. Ticket Consolidators

Airlines know which seats on an overseas flight are unlikely to be bought at the going rates. Some of them dump these seats into the hands of a consolidator, who buys a block of seats on a flight at a fire-sale price. Consolidators resell the seats to the public at discounts of as much as 30 percent. Typically, they sell tickets for international flights rather than for domestic travel.

Buying through a consolidator often lets you get around those annoying advance-purchase requirements. Big travel agencies like Thomas Cook, which warehouses consolidator tickets, will sell a discount fare ticket for a next-day flight—if it has one.

How do you tell a consolidator from a travel agent? The consolidator, who sells directly to the public through newspaper ads, is primarily in the business of selling budget airplane seats. The travel agency is usually a full-service operation that offers not only regular airline-ticketing services, package tours, and bookings for hotels, rental cars, and cruises, but also travel advice and trip planning.

A word of warning: cutting a truly good deal

with consolidators can be tricky. And although savings may be high, so too may be the levels of frustration. Indeed, some consolidator tickets may be more trouble than they're worth.

For example, your seat may be "confirmed" (guaranteed—if you check in at the airport according to the airline's deadlines), "reserved" (not guaranteed by the airline), "wait-listed" (you have a seat only if others on a completely booked flight cancel in advance), or on "standby" status (you'll get a seat only if you wait at the airport gate and some of the passengers with reservations don't show up). A two-letter code on the ticket will tell you if the seat is confirmed— "OK"—or on the wait list—"RQ." According to an advisory from the Better Business Bureau of Metropolitan New York (BBB), the most common complaints about consolidators include problems in obtaining confirmed seats, limited availability of advertised fares, and high cancellation penalties. (You can, of course, encounter the same kind of troubles with an airline.)

But there are other cautions. The BBB has received many complaints about companies that don't issue a ticket until you arrive at the airport and meet with a consolidator representative. Other gripes involve return flights: some consolidators require that customers call 72 hours before they plan to return to find which flights are available. Sometimes the phone lines are continuously busy, and the return trip can cost more than the fare you paid to reach your vacation or business destination.

You can often buy consolidator tickets as much

as 30 days in advance, but sometimes tickets are not available until the last minute. If you run into trouble, you must deal with the consolidator or the travel agent go-between rather than the airline itself.

Before doing business directly with a consolidator, see how it's rated by the Better Business Bureau in the city its office is in (for information about finding the right BBB, see Chapter 7). Note, too, that you can get consolidator tickets through smaller travel agencies that work with independent consolidators. Because the travel agency brings business to the consolidator on a regular basis and presumably deals only with reputable companies, that may give you an added degree of protection.

BOX 4-2

THE AIRLINE MARKETING GAME: LOW-FARE PHANTOMS

Before you make a reservation or buy a ticket, keep this warning in mind: airline advertisements are often confusing and misleading; some use deceptive bait-and-switch tactics that are illegal for other businesses. Let the buyer beware.

In summer 1989, Joel Pangborn, a New Jersey traveler, wanted to get the lowest airfare for a 10-day vacation in Europe. He found a great deal advertised in the newspaper—$199 round-trip to Brussels—and called to make reservations. The fare was available, as long as he returned by June 30. That fit nicely with Pangborn's plans, but there was another catch: although there were plenty of $199 seats available going from JFK to

Brussels, no seats were available for the required return by June 30. No round-trip by June 30, no great $199 fare. No exceptions. Thus, the advertised bargain existed in theory but not in practicality. Pangborn complained, "If they advertise the fare, they should have seats available."

This is not an uncommon experience. People throughout the country have been deceived by airline ads. The problems include bait-and-switch tactics, price quotes that do not include all the costs, failure to include pertinent information about restrictions and availability, and burial of important details in blindingly small-type print.

One customer burned by such ads was Dorothy Abrams. She was the wrong person for an airline to mislead. Her experience and that of numerous other consumers prompted Dorothy's son—New York State Attorney General Robert Abrams—to begin monitoring airline ads in 1988. "We had become distressed by an avalanche of false and deceptive ads on radio, TV, newspapers, and magazines," says Robert Abrams.

Abrams and the National Association of Attorneys General drew up guidelines that tell airlines what they must do to stay within existing law. At first, the airlines cleaned up their act. But with the encouragement of the USDOT, some airlines resumed deceptive advertising.

"The problem is that one or two airlines with a willingness to engage in bait-and-switch advertising have led the entire industry into this practice," says Abrams. "TWA has been the bad actor in this; it's the leader of the pack." In the spring of 1989, TWA and Pan Am were sued in New York State Supreme Court by the AG's office for false advertising.

The Pan Am suit alleges the carrier advertised a "mythical" one-way fare to various Euopean

continued

cities, but the actual cost was more than double that, because the customer had to buy a round-trip ticket. Pending litigation, a Pan Am spokesman had no comment on the allegations. TWA is charged with a series of deceptive ads, including one that offers "London Roundtrip + Hotel + Car = $298." In actuality, Abrams says, "a $298 package deal would cost a minimum of $792—$321 airfare, $450 hotel, and $21 car—and could cost as much as $1,418—$321 airfare, $867 hotel, and $253 for an automatic transmission car." A TWA spokesman said that the airline had no comment on the lawsuit but added that the advertisement cited here was no longer running.

Abrams would have dragged other airlines into court but for a case in Texas in which 14 airlines have sued the state for enforcing its rules against deceptive ads. New York and 32 other states have been drawn in as defendants. The case turns on the issue of federal preemption—the airlines say they are subject only to the federal government's deregulated regulations. The USDOT has been siding with the airlines!

In a different but related dispute between the USDOT and the attorneys general, the USDOT proposed a rule rewrite that would let airlines leave out certain charges and allow misleadingly low advertised fare quotes. Customers would pay a higher price when they actually purchased the tickets.

What can consumers do? Ignore airline promotions—especially those by 14 airlines presently shielded from no-deceptive-advertising rules. Because of the Texas suit, New York has been enjoined from enforcing its regulations against TWA, Pan Am, Continental, and 11 foreign airlines. If you spot deceptive airline advertising, file a complaint with your state attorney general.

For addresses and phone numbers of each state attorney general, see Chapter 7.

You should also file a complaint with the Consumer Affairs Office, I-25, U.S. Department of Transportation, Washington, DC 20590. Do this for the record, so your complaint can be included in the USDOT's annual complaint statistics. Don't expect a lot of sympathy, though. "Ninety-nine percent of the people who complain about advertising are people who didn't read the fine print," says the USDOT's Hoyte Decker, assistant director for consumer affairs.

CHAPTER 5

Flying in Comfort:
Where to Find the Best—and Worst—
In-Flight Service

Finding as low an airfare as possible is a priority for most travelers. But before you grab a low-cost ticket, remember that cut-rate fares frequently inspire cut-rate service.

In today's more competitive air travel marketplace, however, almost anything can happen. Some airlines charge rock-bottom prices for bottom-of-the-barrel service. Other airlines, which consistently provide top-quality cabin service, may be forced to charge the same low price as a cattle-car airline at certain times or in certain markets. Even on the same airplane, some customers get better service than they've bargained for, whereas others get taken. Consequently, consumers who want to fly in comfort *and* pay a low fare must stay on their toes. That means carefully weighing each airline's price *and* quality of service.

To make comparisons easier, think of your purchase decision as the result of a mathematical formula. On every airplane flying in the nineties, a certain number of passengers will find themselves sitting in one of three categories, represented by the following mathematical equations:

Equation 1: $QS < TP$ This situation—in which quality of service (QS) is less than the ticket price (TP)—is the one you want to avoid. Business travelers and others who pay full fare for a last-minute trip on a Grade B airline frequently find themselves in this category.

Equation 2: $QS = TP$. This is the fair deal *minimum* you should aim for. If you're paying a good buck for your ticket, you should be flying in comfort. By the same reasoning, if you're flying cheaply, don't expect to be treated like a king. Under Equation 2, you get what you pay for.

Equation 3: $QS > TP$. Consumers who get better quality service than they pay for are ahead of the game. Although customers should always strive to get *at least* the level of service they're paying for, anomalies in the system make it possible for some customers to get *more* than they pay for. This benefit usually comes at the expense of other customers who have willingly, unwillingly, or ignorantly accepted the terms of Equation 1.

The Best Airlines

Reducing your purchase decision to a formula simplifies the task of calculating which airline offers the best price/quality deal. Using the price-shopping techniques explained in Chapter 4, you should have a clear and objective understanding of the high-to-low range of TPs being charged and whether you're paying top dollar or not. But an important factor is missing: how do you measure QS?

All measures of quality are highly subjective. We measure QS by looking at customer preference statistics. One major source for this information is frequent-flier surveys. If frequent fliers—all too familiar with service levels—like or dislike an airline, *you* probably will too.

In 1987, the International Foundation of Airline Passengers Associations surveyed in detail almost 30,000 frequent fliers around the world who take an average of 14 round-trips per year. These people *know* service quality. Among the questions, the IFAPA asked fliers to vote for the title of most widely preferred airline based on *all* factors, including price, service, comfort, and punctuality.

Three different tallies are assembled here for three different reasons:

1. Airlines preferred by passengers worldwide (Table 5-1). This pits U.S. and foreign carriers against each other to establish a world standard of quality service for international service.

2. Airlines preferred by North American residents (Table 5-2). This again pits U.S. and foreign carriers against each other, but the standard of measure is slightly different, because it reflects the tastes and needs particular to North American residents.

3. North American airlines preferred by North Americans for travel within the continent (Table 5-3). Since roughly 90 percent of U.S. air travel takes place within the continent, this ranks the

airlines *available* to you for domestic travel. (Foreign airlines are barred by treaty agreements from U.S. domestic service and can only fly to and from U.S. cities on their international flights.)

TABLE 5-1

The World's Most Preferred Airlines

Ranked according to rounded percentage of customer votes received. Grouped by similar percentage vote. Ties alphabetized.

Rank	Airline	Percentage of Customer Votes Received
1	Swissair	13%
2	Singapore Airlines	10
3	Lufthansa	7
4	American Airlines	6
5	British Airways	6
6	Delta Air Lines	6
7	KLM	5
8	United Airlines	5
9	Cathay Pacific	4
10	Air France	3
11	Japan Air Lines	3
12	Pan Am	3
13	SAS	3
14	Thai Airlines	3
15	TWA	3
16	Qantas	2
17	Air Canada	1
18	British Caledonia	1
19	Northwest	1
20	Varig	1

Source: IFAPA.

TABLE 5-2

Airlines Most Preferred by North Americans

Ranked according to rounded percentage of customer votes received from North American fliers. Grouped by similar percentage vote. Ties alphabetized.

Rank	Airline	Percentage of Customer Votes Received
1	American Airlines	12%
2	Delta Air Lines	11
3	Swissair	9
4	United Airlines	8
5	Singapore Airlines	6
6	TWA	6
7	British Airways	5
8	Lufthansa	5
9	KLM	4
10	Pan Am	4
11	SAS	3
12	Air Canada	2
13	Air France	2
14	Cathay Pacific	2
15	Japan Air Lines	2
16	Northwest	2
17	Qantas	2
18	British Caledonia	1
19	Thai Airlines	1
20	Varig	1

Source: IFAPA.

TABLE 5-3

Top 10 Major North American Airlines, Preference Order

Ranked according to rounded percentage of customer votes received from North American fliers. Non-North American airlines excluded. Ties alphabetized.

Rank	Airline	Percentage of Customer Votes Received
1	American Airlines	26%
2	Delta Air Lines	23
3	United	18
4	TWA	7
5	Eastern	5
6	Northwest	4
7	Air Canada	3
8	Continental	3
9	Piedmont	3
10	Pan Am	1

Source: IFAPA.

In the first tally, the two most preferred airlines by a significant margin worldwide were Swissair and Singapore Airlines. American and Delta were the most preferred U.S. carriers among the world's travelers. The second ranking of airlines, by North American residents only, is slightly different, with American and Delta topping the list. There is general agreement with world residents on which airlines were among the top 10. The third list, confined to North Americans voting for the top 10 major North American airlines, is not a true most-preferred list, because there are only nine major U.S. airlines. American, Delta, and United are significantly preferred over other

North American carriers. Conspicuously absent from the list is USAir—one of the nine majors.

Once you have the ticket price (TP) and quality service QS information in hand, you can make an informed decision by following these three simple rules of thumb:

If the available airlines' TPs are equal, choose the airline with the higher QS rating. For example, using Table 5-3, suppose American and Northwest were charging the same fare for a particular flight. Which airline should you choose? We'd pick American, which has the higher QS rating.

If the available airlines have similar QS ratings, choose the airline with the lower TP. Thus if you had a choice between Air Canada and Continental, which have similar QS ratings, but Continental was charging a lower fare, fly with Continental.

If neither TP nor QS are equal at the available airlines, choose the factor—lowest TP or highest QS—that is most important to you. Say high-QS Delta is charging $150 for a one-way ticket and low-QS Pan Am is charging $100. In this case, you have to examine your own preferences very carefully. If you're on a tight budget, the $50 savings may be worth the greater *potential* that you'll have a less pleasant flight on Pan Am; if you want better service and are willing to pay more for it, the choice is clear: Delta.

You carry out these kinds of purchase decisions all the time, whether you're in the supermarket, an automobile showroom, or a realtor's office. Knowing each airline's QS is the key to making an informed choice.

The Complaint File

Customers lodge complaints about everything from rude flight attendants, poor cabin service, and horrible food to late flights, deceptive advertising, and long lines at the ticket counter. Therefore, another way to gauge the QS factor is to look at how many complaints the USDOT receives about each airline per 100,000 passengers.

The USDOT constantly tracks the complaint record of each airline and produces monthly and annual tallies available to the public in the "Air Travel Consumer Report." (For free copies of the monthly reports, write to: Office of Consumer Affairs, U.S. Department of Transportation, 400 7th Street, SW, Room 10405, Washington, DC 20590.)

Table 5-4 ranks the large U.S. airlines' service from worst-to-best based on the number of complaints per 100,000 passengers. An airline that appears high on the complaint list is providing a lower quality of service than other airlines receiving fewer complaints. Three large airlines (Eastern, Pan Am, TWA) and tiny Tower Air top the list.

Two giants, Delta and American, rank near the bottom of the complaint list, meaning they are keeping customers happy. That correlates closely with the IFAPA preference list. Two smaller airlines, Air Wisconsin and Aloha, had the smallest number of complaints per 100,000 passengers.

TABLE 5-4

Complaints Against U.S. Airlines

Ranked worst-to-best, based on the number of complaints filed with the USDOT per 100,000 passengers in 1989.

Rank	Airline	Complaints per 100,000 Passengers
1	Eastern	6.5
2	Pan Am	6.1
3	TWA	5.3
4	Tower Air	5.3
5	Hawaiian Airlines	4.2
6	Braniff	4.2
7	Continental	3.3
AVERAGE		2.2
8	Piedmont	2.2
9	USAir	2.1
10	United	2.0
11	Northwest	2.0
12	Midway	1.6
13	America West	1.4
14	American Trans Air	1.3
15	American Airlines	1.2
16	Alaska Airlines	0.9
17	Southwest	0.8
18	Delta Air Lines	0.7
19	Horizon Airlines	0.6
20	Aloha Airlines	0.3
21	Air Wisconsin	0.3

Source: USDOT.

The information contained in this table is updated regularly in *Ready for Take-off Database*, a quarterly publication. For subscription information, write to: *Ready for Take-off Database*, P.O. Box 521, Easton, PA 18044-0521.

More Than Meets the Eye

Don't be fooled by the small complaint numbers. Eastern's 6.5 complaints per 100,000 customers *do* look minuscule in absolute terms. But the absolute number is not as important as the number of complaints *relative* to what other airlines are getting. A complaint rate of 6.5 is almost *three times* the average; it's more than *nine times* Delta's rate! That doesn't happen by accident. Complaint rates bear an inverse relationship to QS; the higher the quality of service, the lower the number of complaints.

To translate the true meaning of the complaint file and to compare complaint rates properly, Ready for Take-off grades each airline based on its relative complaint rate. The airline with the lowest complaint rate receives a grade of 100; the average complaint rate equals a grade of 75. This top range establishes our grading scale, or standard of excellence. Airlines that score below average QS are graded accordingly.

Thus, Aloha Airlines and Air Wisconsin both score QS grades of 100, with their rates of 0.3 complaints per 100,000 passengers. In other words, when *all* factors are considered, Aloha and Air Wisconsin did the best job serving their customers that any airline could have possibly done that year, given such immeasurable constraints as cost limits, competitive pressures, and even customer tastes.

The average rate of 2.2 complaints per 100,000 equals 75. Consequently, each .076 drop in the rate of complaints per 100,000 pushes the QS grade *up* 1 point. Viewed like this, it is much easier to see which airlines are at the head of their class and which poor performers are flunking out. Table 5-5 shows the full report card.

READY FOR TAKE-OFF

TABLE 5-5

Airline Service Quality Report Card, 1989

Graded best-to-worst based on the number of complaints the USDOT received about each airline per 100,000 passengers, with the smallest complaint rate earning the highest grade.

Airline	QS Grade	
Air Wisconsin	100%	Grade A
Aloha Airlines	100	
Horizon Airlines	96	
Delta Air Lines	95	
Southwest	94	
Alaska Airlines	92	
American Airlines	88	Grade B
American Trans Air	87	
America West	86	
Midway	83	
Northwest	78	Grade C
United	78	
USAir	77	
Piedmont	75	
		Grade D
Continental	61	Fail
Braniff	49	
Hawaiian Airlines	49	
Tower Air	35	
TWA	35	
Pan Am	23	
Eastern	18	

Source: Flight Control Database, USDOT.

The information contained in this table is updated regularly in *Ready for Take-off Database*, a quarterly publication. For subscription information, write to: *Ready for Take-off Database*, P.O. Box 521, Easton, PA 18044-0521.

Happy Workers = Good Service

What makes one airline better than the rest?

Good service begins with employees who are well-paid and treated with respect by their employers. That requires a smart management team that has earned the respect of its employees and demonstrated it knows how to run an airline.

There is a strong correlation between labor costs, the quality of service, and the profitability of the airline. "The more you pay people, the more motivated the work force is," says one industry analyst. "American and Delta are two of the highest paying airlines and they're the two most profitable." Salaries at Swissair, another top-rated airline, are at the high end too.

Table 5-6 shows the starting pay per flight hour that airlines pay flight attendants, who are on the frontlines of cabin service and the people most likely to influence your opinion of whether the airline is friendly or unfriendly, helpful or unhelpful. QS grades from Table 5-5 are also noted on the table to show the relationship between salary and QS.

Among U.S. carriers, 38.9 percent of Delta's costs and 34.3 percent of American's go to labor, according to Airline Economics, a Washington-based consulting firm. Compare that to 30.9 percent at Pan Am and 22.8 percent at Continental.

Simply put, happy workers make happy customers.

TABLE 5-6

Where Would You Want to Work?

Flight attendant starting salaries per flight hour at major U.S. airlines as of December, 1990, ranked highest to lowest, and QS grade based on Table 5-5.

Airline	Flight Attendant starting salary per flight hour	QS Grade
Delta	$22.80	A
American	16.07	B
United	15.98	C
TWA	15.50	F
Pan Am	15.38	F
Northwest	15.06	C
USAir	14.60	C
Eastern	14.30	F
Continental	14.00	F

Source: *Ready for Takeoff*, airline information.

Smart Management Makes Happy Customers

The importance of a management team that knows how to run an airline cannot be overstressed either, particularly in the area of labor/management relations. You're more likely to encounter unfriendly, unenthused service at an airline where the labor/management relations are rocky. "When you have unhappy employees, there's no way they don't reflect that in everyday service to the consumer," says Henry Duffy, president of the Airline Pilots Association.

The labor/management conflicts at Continental and Eastern are well known. Relations are fair at USAir, says Morgan Stanley & Co. stock analyst Kevin Murphy. "American's, Delta's, and Southwest's labor relations are very good. Pan Am's and TWA's are improving," he states.

Northwest had rocky labor/management relations in the wake of its 1986 merger with Republic Airlines, and the airline's QS suffered. Northwest Chairman Alfred Checchi, who bought the airlines in 1989, understands the relationship between happy workers and good service and accepts management responsibility for improving labor relations. So he has been mending fences and getting acquainted with the airline's 40,000 employees by meeting with small groups of 40 to 50 workers at a time. That work is part of Checchi's overall plan to improve Northwest's QS.

United Airlines is a special case. Labor/management tensions have been rising there, but the employees have also been attempting to buy the company. Assuming they are successful in obtaining financing, United will be an important test case of how employee ownership can affect customers. It won't all be a bowl of cherries, however, because someone—in this instance, a professional manager from outside the company who has already been chosen—will ultimately have to run the airline and make tough decisions. Some of those tough calls will almost certainly be detrimental to employees. Thus at United, as at every other company, management must still know how to communicate, persuade, compromise, and work with the employees.

Admittedly, it's a tough balancing act. Managers have to be firm without clubbing employees over the head; they must do what's best for the company while considering and tempering the negative impact on employees; they must see the company as a team effort of employees *and* management (with management leading the way), rather than as an adversarial relationship.

The managers of Continental, Eastern, TWA, and Pan Am have been slow to demonstrate such skills, and it shows in those airlines' poor QS report cards. Pan Am Chairman and CEO Thomas Plaskett admitted as much in 1990. "Pan Am became so involved with its corporate problems that it lost sight of its customers' needs," he said. Texas Air Corp. Chairman Frank Lorenzo learned he had flunked the hard way. After Texas Air subsidiary Eastern Airlines suffered a gut-wrenching strike and more than $1.2 billion in losses in 12 months of bankruptcy, Federal bankruptcy court Judge Burton Lifland wrested control of Eastern away from Lorenzo in 1990, saying, "Eastern's owner/manager as personified by [Lorenzo] is not competent to reorganize this estate." Judge Lifland went on to say that Texas Air's treatment of its Eastern subsidiary "is suggestive of parental neglect." In summer 1990, Lorenzo stepped down as chairman of Texas Air (now Continental Airlines Holdings) and sold his share of the company to Scandanavian Airline System

Other managers, however, seem to have natural talent for running an airline. Swissair's employees are loyal because of good labor/management relations. "We've never gone through those hiring and firing practices of other airlines—hiring 1,000 people in good times, then firing 1,500 in bad times," says Mark Ellinger, Swissair's full-fare product manager. Indeed, in 1988 Swissair took a sharp pencil to administrative costs, reducing nine layers of *management* to six.

Delta's esprit de corps is legendary, despite some friction from the merger of Western Airlines' unionized work force into the nonunion Delta family. "Delta is almost like a cult. Management is very paternalistic. It's a traditional Southern airline," says one expert.

So dedicated are Delta employees, in 1982 they *gave* the airline a gift—a Boeing 767 jet—paid for with their own voluntary contributions. The employees wanted to thank management for an 8.5 percent pay increase (despite the airline's $18.4 million first-quarter 1982 loss) and for their job security in an industry in which some 40,000 employees lose their jobs. The gift "is a dramatic, visible expression of an invisible spirit," New York Stock Exchange Chairman William Batten told *Reader's Digest*. "It shows that Delta employees identify their personal well-being with the company well-being. It's not a we–they attitude, but us together. What a symbol this is to American business."

Not only are Delta's employees top drawer, but management also has its head on straight. "Look, when you're moving 60 million people a year, things will go wrong. How you handle those situations is what makes the difference," says Delta vice president Al Kolakoski. "Our people respond to everyday problems. We don't treat the customer with indifference. Nine times out of ten we turn a complaint experience into a pleasant one."

The Big Picture

Smart management and a good labor/management relationship are key to just about everything that makes happy consumers. Flip through the numerous ratings tables throughout this book. You will find the same two to four well-run airlines consistently at or near the top.

Look at profitability, safety records, customer satisfaction, baggage handling, on-time performance. The same names keep rising to the top. It's no fluke; it's good management.

Fine-Tuning Your Flight Comfort

Although flying with an overall top-rated airline will give you an excellent shot at a pleasant flight experience, you can fine-tune your comfort level even further by more closely examining specific elements of the service—roominess of the seats, food service, on-time performance, baggage handling, and overbooking/cancellation problems.

You can exert a degree of control over these factors by carefully choosing your airline. The first two—seating comfort and food—are covered in this chapter. Fine-tuning the remaining service factors will be covered in Chapter 6.

The Best Seats

Everyone wants a comfortable roomy seat, but most people don't find out they've got a cramped seat until they're already on the plane. By then it's too late; who will trundle against the stream of inflowing passengers, off the plane, and back out to a ticket counter to endure the hassle of changing a seat assignment?

The trick to getting a comfortable seat—as with everything else—is advance planning. Thanks to a little-known publication called *The Airline Seating Guide,* it's possible to "see" what you're headed for before you buy your tickets. "Since deregulation, airline seating has gotten tighter and tighter," says Monty Stanford, the 6 foot 1 inch editor who founded the guide.

Most passengers don't know it, but airlines can move their seats around on a plane, either forcing them closer together to get more seats on the plane or spacing them for more room. This reconfiguration goes on all the time. Roughly 30 percent of the aircraft covered by Stanford's guide are reconfigured quarterly.

Different airlines put different numbers of seats on the same-type plane. Continental's 737-200 has 102 seats, whereas Aloha Airline's setup on the 737-200 has 116 seats—more seats, less room. Lufthansa has 22 roomy first-class seats on its DC-10-30; United, meanwhile, scrunches 40 first-class seats into the same space. People Express used to really pack 'em in. Typically, there are 400 to 430 seats on a 747. "People Express had 490 to 500 seats," recalls Stanford.

To get the best seats, start by asking the ticket agent what kind of equipment—DC-10, B-747, A300—is assigned to the flight. This information is also available on the Official Airline Guide Electronic Edition. Be sure you get as specific a model number as possible. The Boeing 727-100 is a 133-foot plane that can seat approximately 118 passengers; the Boeing 727-200, essentially the same as the B-727-100, is 153 feet long because of the insertion of a "plug"—an extra 20-foot section of fuselage. With the added length, the B-727-200 can handle roughly 30 percent more seats than the B-727-100.

Once you know what kind of plane you'll most likely be flying on—though equipment changes *are* possible before boarding—you can use *The Airline Seating Guide* to view a seating diagram of the plane. Knowing the lay of the land will allow you to plan. The guide shows how many seats are packed into each row, and which seat letters designate aisle, window, or middle seats. It also notes seats and rows with the most and least legroom when available, seats that don't recline, Airfone availability and locations, and seats from which you can't see the movie. Want to be close to an exit? Do you hate being seated near the hustle and bustle of the galley or the lavatories? The guide will help you plan. You can even map out seating so you're among the first served the in-flight meal and you're not stuck at the end of the line with a limited choice of entrée.

Four quarterly issues of the guide cost $39.95 for the U.S. edition and $44.95 for the overseas edition. Write to: Carlson Publishing Co., P.O. Box 888, Los Alamitos, CA 90720.

Airline Food

You know an airline is good when customers even like the—eeeech!—food. Some passengers actually write and request the recipes for items like Delta Air Line's fried sesame chicken breast, ham cartwheels, and baked stuffed apples.

Air travel pragmatists might think the quality of food served at 30,000 feet is a relatively unimportant issue. After all, when you book passage on an airplane, you're buying fast transportation, not a table at The Four Seasons. In fact, "food is extremely important. A meal takes up part of the boring time you spend in a plane," says Phillip Cooke, executive administrator of the Inflight Food Service Association. Captives on a 3- to 7-hour nonstop flight get hungry, and the airplane galley is the only restaurant in town. When Eastern Airlines began flying into financial difficulties, it "cut food to the bone and didn't think customers would notice," says Cooke. "But it was just one more negative perception for the consumer."

In the airline food business, the sands are always shifting. Experts say the quality of airline food moves in cycles. When passengers demand low airfares, food service suffers; when passengers want better cabin service, the airlines pay more attention to food.

How can you find good food in the air? Here are some rules of thumb:

Right now, customers want better cabin service, and the airlines are listening. Food has gained importance at all the airlines in the nineties, after early-deregulation fare wars sparked culinary cutbacks. Part of the new emphasis is on creative cold foods for coach-class passengers. "Delta, American, and United are taking the lead in giving customers innovative, fun food," says Cooke. "Delta has a cream soup and pita that customers love."

Cold foods are not necessarily cheaper, but they're quicker to deliver on today's more common short-hop flight. It's also easier to maintain consistent quality with cold food: while passengers are fuming over delayed departures, reheated food sitting in the galley quickly turns into yesterday's leftovers.

Don't put much stock in awards, food critic choices, and airline ads gushing about the great food, unless you're flying first class, because these backslappers generally concern the first-class menu—not the selection available in coach, where most passengers fly. Learn where attention to the palate is greatest. U.S. airlines put greater emphasis on their transoceanic food service because of the long duration of the flights and competition from foreign carrier chefs.

In general, the regulated airlines of European and Asian countries with economic and industrial might serve better food than U.S. carriers, because service is king in those countries. In the United States, price and service constantly battle each other, with low prices frequently winning out to the detriment of quality service. On Swissair, for example, even economy-class meals are served on china, not plastic and Styrofoam. In business class, the meal is served in separate courses. And, except for champagne in economy class, all drinks are free.

Some small U.S. carriers have found a niche providing top-quality food and cabin service. Midwest Express serves meals to its all-coach passengers on china and crystal glassware. The food typically served on Midwest Express is atypical too—lobster, braised grouse, and fricassee of oyster.

To meet the competition, some major U.S. airlines are dishing out more lavish spreads internationally and on some domestic flights. The biggest improvements are being made for passengers flying business and first class.

One indicator of good airline food is how much each airline spends on food per passenger. Midwest Express, for example, spends an average $9.50 per passenger, versus an industry average of $5.35 per passenger. Table 5-7 ranks food

TABLE 5-7

Champagne—or Beer—Budget?

Major-airline expenditures on in-flight food per passenger in 1989, ranked highest to lowest.

Airline	Food Expenditure per Passenger
Pan Am	$6.99
TWA	6.17
American	6.03
United	5.83
Northwest	4.85
Continental	4.80
Delta	4.73
Eastern	4.36
USAir	4.29

Source: Airline Economics.

spending per passenger by the major airlines. Pan Am tops the list by a significant margin, spending $6.99 per passenger. USAir winds up on the bottom, at $4.29—primarily because its concentration on short-haul flights doesn't allow time for more than simple foods.

Another way you can improve the quality—and possibly the nutritional value—of your in-flight food is to order special meals. Although they don't much publicize it, most airlines will provide special food at no extra charge. Obtain information about available special menu items and order when you make your reservations. What kind of food is available? The offerings vary from airline to airline and flight to flight, but in general, people with special dietary restrictions can order meals that are low-calorie, low-sodium, or low-cholesterol. Kosher and vegetarian meals are widely available, and Hindu and Moslem fare are gaining popularity. If you're on a seafood, fruit, or bland diet, most airlines will accommodate you.

But of all the special meals available, perhaps the most important is the children's menu—hot dogs, hamburgers, milk, and cookies, in lieu of the adult concoctions many children simply won't touch.

BOX 5-1

THE AIRLINE MARKETING GAME: HANDCUFFING THE FREQUENT FLIER

Brand loyalty is a consumer phenomenon every company tries to develop. The best way to get *genuine* brand loyalty is to produce a product that's better than everyone else's. Airline frequent-flier programs were designed to create *artificial brand loyalty*. The purpose is to keep passengers—particularly businesspeople—flying the same airline so they can rack up mileage and collect free plane tickets.

We recommend you ignore this marketing gimmick for at least six good reasons:

1. *Frequent-flier program members sell themselves into captivity.* Because a company typically pays for the tickets of an employee frequent flier, the dollar cost for the flying beneficiary is zero. Since you have to be on some flight anyway, earning frequent-flier mileage costs you nothing in time, either. What could be better than getting something for nothing?

Think carefully about that. How often do you get something for nothing anywhere?

What an airline is really purchasing through a frequent-flier program is your consumer freedom of choice to switch airlines. As mileage builds in your account, you have a greater and greater incentive *to accept poor service* from the airline.

Frequent-flier programs are designed to buy your right to vote for a better-quality competitor. That in turn erodes your power as a customer. In today's competitive marketplace, no frequent-flier bonus is worth that cost.

continued

2. *Comparisons between programs are difficult, if not impossible.* Bonus points, minimum mileage awards, restrictions, mileage expiration deadlines, and numerous other details are different at each airline. This means no rational comparisons can be made—a crucial element in every marketing strategy. That opens the door for the airline advertiser to "help" the customer and "explain" why its program is the best.

3. *The airlines can change their frequent-flier program rules at anytime without notice—or terminate the program altogether.* "That means miles earned by a frequent flier are at risk of being devalued at any time," says Rhonda Singer, general counsel of the Better Business Bureau of Metropolitan New York.

Sound unlikely that you could get burned? Airline accountants and stock analysts are now beginning to look more closely at the growing balance sheet *liability* of more than 600 billion unused miles accruing in these programs. Many corporations have walked away from their pension fund liabilities in recent years; how much easier would it be for an airline to walk away from a burdensome and easily erasable marketing liability?

4. *Restrictions frequently apply to frequent-flyer free tickets.* "There can be quotas on the number of frequent fliers allowed on a given bonus flight, or blackout dates when the bonus ticket cannot be used," warns New York State Attorney General Robert Abrams.

5. *Finding your way through the airline maze and getting good service is complicated enough.* Factoring myriad details about frequent-flier programs into the equation adds unnecessary complexity. Entire books are devoted to frequent-flier program minutiae. If you enjoy plowing through confusing rules

and fine print, go fill out your income tax forms instead.

6. *Frequent-flier programs divert your attention from more important factors in the airline ticket purchase decision—airfares, service quality, on-time performance, safety.* In some cases, an impending award could cause you to stick with an inferior airline—just so you can get a free ticket for more inferior service. A bargain, that's not.

CHAPTER 6

Avoiding the Major Hassles:
Late or Canceled Flights, Overbooked Planes,
Bungled Baggage

Good cabin service, friendly flight attendants, roomy seats, and good food are only part of what an airline should do for its customers. The airline should also get you to your destination or connecting flight on time; if it sells you a ticket it should have a seat on the plane for you; and at the end of the flight it should reunite you with your baggage in timely fashion. All too often, though, airlines don't meet these basic standards of service. When that happens, passengers aren't just shortchanged getting the service they've paid for, they must then face a major hassle:

• James Davidson, chairman of the National Taxpayers Union, had to be in Fort Lee, NJ, for a 1:30 P.M. taping of the CNBC TV show "McLaughlin." He arrived at Washington's National Airport in plenty of time to catch Continental's 11 A.M. shuttle to Newark. But the partially full shuttle didn't leave at 11 A.M.—because of air traffic control problems, recalls Davidson. It didn't leave at noon either. Meanwhile, more passengers arrived at the gate. Finally, at 12:15 the flight began boarding. Even with the merger of three flights—11 A.M., 12 P.M., and 1 P.M.—the plane was still only partially filled, says Davidson. It finally took off at 12:40. Davidson was late, the TV show's producers were frantic, and the taping session had to be redone at a cost of thousands of dollars. Continental, meanwhile, saved money by making one late flight instead of three separate ones.

• After flying from Mexico City to Kansas City, Wylene Heninger, a teacher and writer from Colorado Springs, CO, waited for her luggage at the baggage carousel. She waited for more than an hour as other passengers retrieved their luggage. Heninger's bag, however, was nowhere to be seen. Airline personnel told her the bag had been misplaced, and she received it that evening. But the story doesn't end there. Heninger opened the bag only to find it full of a priest's robes. The airline returned the wrong bag, meaning that somewhere, a second defrocked passenger's luggage was now misplaced. Finally, two days after her arrival and a quarter of the way through her vacation— Heninger got the right bag.

• Robert Foley, a New York communications analyst, may be the only victim to have had the last laugh. He had tickets on United to Chicago, but the airline had overbooked the flight—sold tickets to more passengers than it had seats for on the plane. Foley volunteered to give up his seat in exchange for an additional free round-trip ticket to the destination of his choice. Another passenger immediately offered Foley $200 for the free ticket and Foley sold it. Then he watched with amazement as the flight he was bumped from pushed away from the gate, stopped, then returned to the terminal with mechanical problems. Foley arrived in Chicago on another flight a full hour before the flight he was bumped from.

Air travel problems like Davidson's, Heninger's, and Foley's are not isolated incidents. In 1989, airlines involuntarily bumped 110,497 fare-paying customers. They mishandled more than 3 million pieces of luggage. Some 1.6 million flights carrying an estimated 108 million passengers arrived late.

You need not become a victim of poor airline service. By taking control and becoming a responsible, educated consumer, you can increase your chances of avoiding the major hassles. It's a simple, three-step process:

1. Learn which airlines provide good service and reward only the best carriers with your business.
2. Know your contractual and legal rights.
3. Practice a handful of hassle-avoidance techniques to keep even the best airlines from botching up.

On-Time Performance

One major service the U.S. Department of Transportation provides to consumers is a detailed statistical data base of the on-time performance of major air carriers. Each month, airlines are required to provide the USDOT with computer tapes containing information about every flight. While you *can* purchase these tapes for use on your own mainframe computer, you can get your hands on a much more practical distillation of the information produced by the USDOT, the "Air Travel Consumer Report." Each month, the report shows what percentage of each airline's flights arrived on time and lists specific flights that arrived late more than 80 percent of the time. (The monthly report is available free to consumers. To request a copy, write to: Office of Consumer Affairs, U.S. Department of Transportation, 400 7th Street, SW, Room 10405, Washington, DC 20590.)

Because the top performers can change from month to month, *Ready for Take-off* looks at consistent long-term performance. Table 6-1 shows the long-term performance of reporting carriers for the period beginning September 1987 (when USDOT record keeping began) through March 1990.

The most dependably prompt carriers nationwide were America West, Southwest, and American, arriving as scheduled 80 to 84 percent of the time. Among the majors, American leads the pack by a much longer shot than is evident from the cumulative numbers. To see why, you have to examine the month-by-month data.

In the 31 months between September 1987, and March 1990, American was first among the majors in on-time performance 35 percent of the time. No other major airline comes close.* (Delta and Pan Am, the closest contenders, each came

*Eastern Airlines *did* rack up an impressive monthly first-place streak between September 1988 and September 1989, but the record was a fluke. The move to first place resulted from a

TABLE 6-1

Better Late Than Never . . .

Tardiness of the largest U.S. national and regional airlines ranked best-to-worst in terms of percentage of flights arriving late from September 1987, through March 1990.

Rank	Airline	Percentage of Late Arrivals
1	America West	16.1%
2	Southwest	17.1
3	American	19.2
4	Alaska Airlines	21.5
5	Delta	21.6
6	Eastern	21.6
	AVERAGE	21.9
7	Continental	22.0
8	Northwest	23.0
9	TWA	23.3
10	Pan Am	24.5
11	United	25.8
12	USAir	26.5

Source: USDOT.

The information contained in this table is updated regularly in *Ready for Take-off Database*, a quarterly publication. For subscription information, write to: *Ready for Take-off Database*, P.O. Box 521, Easton, PA 18044-0521.

---

drastic downscaling of Eastern's operations because of poor management, financial problems, and disastrous labor/management relations.

Eastern's good showing against the majors came when the airline essentially became a puddle jumper. The carrier reduced service from 81 cities in early 1988 to just 8 in May 1989. As flights were cut back, on-time performance soared. In 1989, Eastern began to rebuild its schedule, and, as it climbed back into the major leagues, unexceptional on-time performance levels returned.

in first for the month 10 percent of the time.) What that says loud and clear is that getting passengers to the gate on time is a serious priority at American, it's not just marketing hyperbole.

The story at United Airlines is slightly different. That carrier advertises itself as dedicated to giving business flyers what they want most. There are few things business travelers value more than an airline that gets them to their meetings on time. Yet United apparently doesn't get it. In 31 months, The Friendly Skies never came in first in on-time performance. In more than a few months, United was the *latest* among the majors, sinking to a 41 percent-late record in December 1989.

Big Difference, or Small?

Look at the on-time performance of Northwest Airlines (23 percent of its flights are late) and American (19.2 percent of its flights are late). The spread between the two is less than four points. Is that tiny number really worth crowing about?

Yes, for two reasons. First, that difference means you're almost 20 percent more likely to be late flying Northwest than you would be flying American. Compare USAir (26.5 percent late) and America West (16.1 percent late), and you've got a 65 percent greater chance of arriving late if you fly USAir. For our money, these kinds of differentials are worth considering. The tiny 5 percent differential between TWA and Pan Am, on the other hand, may not be worth arguing over.

Second, these differences represent a tangible measure of the airline's commitment to on-time performance, in much the same way a straight-A student must be more dedicated than an A's-and-B's student. American's long-term record is not just luck of the draw.

An airline's commitment to on-time performance differs from airport to airport based on how important a particular market is to the airline. For example, to Eastern Airlines, which was rebuilding its route network in 1989 after a debilitating strike, the Atlanta hub was key to the airline's rebirth. Half of Eastern's 14,000-plus flights per month were landing at Atlanta by December. So Eastern gave Atlanta full attention, and only 15 percent of its flights landing there in 1989 arrived late, versus 19 percent systemwide. San Francisco, on the other hand, with only 80 flights per month by December, was clearly off the beaten path for Eastern. There, 39 percent of Eastern flights arriving in 1989 were late.

Similar relationships can even be found at American. Dallas-Ft. Worth is a major hub for American Airlines, and in 1989 only 16 percent of the airline's arrivals at DFW were late. Los Angeles is another big market for American, and in 1989 only 19 percent of American's arrivals there were late. Phoenix and Minneapolis-St. Paul, conversely—two significantly smaller markets for American—don't manage the same levels of on-time performance. At both cities in 1989, 26 percent of American's arrivals were late.

This is *not* to say that either airline is not as

committed to smaller cities as it is to larger markets. The point is this: inside corporate headquarters, each airline has a secret priority listing of its destinations. When it comes time to apportion operating expenses, manpower, and capital investment resources to each airport, some are farther at the front of the line and some are toward the back. If you could determine which are which, you could reduce your chances of flying a particular airline to a low-priority city. You could choose a competing airline more committed to the destination, and you might even get better service all around, since an airline's commitment to serving a particular market affects all aspects of service.

But how can you determine which cities are very important and which are not so important to each airline? One way is to keep abreast of goings-on at the airlines by reading *The Wall Street Journal* or the business pages of a major or national daily. One person flying Eastern from the New York area to Sarasota was casually aware of Eastern's Atlanta strategy from news reports. She had a hunch she'd be better off flying from Newark to Sarasota via a connecting flight through Atlanta. She arrived on time.

Flying the exact same day were two friends of hers who, however, wanted the convenience and speed of a direct flight. For this, they had to fly Eastern from New York's LaGuardia Airport to Sarasota. They left an hour earlier and arrived in Sarasota 2 hours after the woman on the Newark-Atlanta-Sarasota flight. On the return, the Sarasota-Atlanta-Newark flight was again on time. The Sarasota-LaGuardia flight was canceled because of mechanical problems and the couple had to take a later flight—through Atlanta. They arrived 4 hours after their originally scheduled direct flight should have arrived.

Another way to divine the importance of a particular destination to an airline is to follow the money trail. If an airline does a lot of business to a destination, it will usually devote plenty of attention to keeping the planes moving and the money spigot flowing freely. Ask the ticket agent how many gates the airline has at your destination or if the airport serves as one of the airline's hubs. Unfortunately, this gauge does not always provide an exact reading. You can't *always* assume that just because a city serves as a hub for a particular airline that its on-time performance there will be great. Philadelphia, for example, is an important USAir hub, yet in 1989, 32 percent of USAir arrivals there were late.

The best way to see which cities the major airlines are committed to and which they care much less about is to look at the on-time performance over the previous 12 months airport by airport and airline by airline.

Ready for Take-off analyzed the USDOT on-time arrival data of the nine biggest carriers at 29 major U.S. airports in 1989. Box 6-1 shows the 10 cities to which each airline is most committed to delivering on-time service. Only on-time performance records above the 76 percent average for 1989 are listed, so some airlines have fewer than 10 destinations listed. If the airline can't distinguish itself by delivering even slightly above-average performance, it can't be overly dedicated to that destination.

Box 6-2 shows the major carriers' least important destinations from among the nation's 29 biggest airports, based on the percentage of flights arriving there late in 1989. Only destinations where 35 percent or more of the airline's flights were late are counted.

If you're flying to one of the 29 major airports listed, use the information in Box 6-1 to find which airline does an exemplary job to that airport. In some cases, more than one airline has a commendable on-time record to the destination. Choose the one or two with the highest on-time percentage.

Four airports—Newark, New York's JFK, Chicago's O'Hare, and San Francisco—don't show up in Box 6-1 because no one airline does a super job getting to those overburdened airports on time. However, the best performers at those busy airports in 1989 were TWA (77 percent) and American (75 percent) at Newark; American (79 percent) at JFK; TWA (74 percent) at O'Hare; and American (74 percent) at San Francisco.

Use Box 6-2 to protect yourself from especially bad service by certain airlines to certain destinations.

BOX 6-1

Committed to Timely Service

If you're flying to any of the cities cited below, these airlines will likely do the best job getting you there promptly. Listed here are the major airline's 10 most important destinations and the percentage of their flights arriving there on time in 1989. This list is drawn from on-time performance statistics for 29 major U.S. airports. Only above-average (76 percent) performance counts, so some airlines have fewer than 10 destinations listed. Airlines are ranked in order of each one's "On-time score"—the total number of above-average on-time percentage points.

Continental Airlines   On-time score: 831

1. Washington Dulles (86%)
2. Las Vegas (85%)
3. Minneapolis-St. Paul (84%)
4. Dallas-Ft. Worth (84%)
5. Houston Intercont. (83%)
6. Kansas City (83%)
7. Phoenix (83%)
8. Philadelphia (82%)
9. Salt Lake City (81%)
10. Denver (80%)

Eastern Airlines   On-time score: 823

1. Atlanta (85%)
2. Washington National (85%)
3. Tampa (85%)
4. Orlando (84%)
5. Pittsburgh (83%)
6. Charlotte-Douglas (82%)
7. Seattle (82%)
8. Detroit (79%)
9. Miami (79%)
10. Philadelphia (79%)

Northwest Airlines On-time score: 815

1. Pittsburgh (84%)
2. Washington Dulles (84%)
3. Houston Intercont. (84%)
4. Kansas City (83%)
5. Memphis (83%)
6. Minneapolis (81%)
7. Detroit (80%)
8. Philadelphia (80%)
9. St. Louis (78%)
10. Atlanta (78%)

American Airlines On-time score: 812

1. Memphis (84%)
2. Dallas-Ft. Worth (84%)
3. Atlanta (82%)
4. Los Angeles (81%)
5. Charlotte-Douglas (81%)
6. Miami (80%)
7. Pittsburgh (80%)
8. Washington Dulles (80%)
9. Tampa (80%)
10. Houston Intercont. (80%)

Delta Air Lines On-time score: 807

1. Kansas City (84%)
2. Pittsburgh (84%)
3. Washington Dulles (83%)
4. Salt Lake City (82%)
5. Memphis (80%)
6. Orlando (80%)
7. Atlanta (79%)
8. Los Angeles (79%)
9. Detroit (78%)
10. Houston Intercont. (78%)

TWA On-time score: 792

1. Memphis (83%)
2. Atlanta (80%)
3. St. Louis (80%)
4. Washington Dulles (79%)
5. Minneapolis (79%)
6. Dallas-Ft. Worth (79%)
7. Philadelphia (78%)
8. Houston Intercont. (78%)
9. Detroit (78%)
10. Tampa (78%)

continued

Pan Am   On-time score: 553

1. San Diego (82%)   5. NY LaGuardia
2. Seattle (81%)   (78%)
3. Boston (80%)   6. Tampa (77%)
4. Houston Intercont.   7. Washington Dulles
   (78%)   (77%)

USAir   On-time score: 235

1. Las Vegas (79%)   2. Washington Dulles
                           (79%)
                        3. Los Angeles (77%)

United Airlines   On-time score: 78

1. Washington Dulles
   (78%)

Source: *Ready for Take-off Database*, USDOT.

The information contained in this box is updated regularly in *Ready for Take-off Database*, a quarterly publication. For subscription information, write to: *Ready for
Take-off Database*, P.O. Box 521, Easton, PA 18044-0521.

BOX 6-2

Laggards

If you're flying to any of the cities cited below,
these airlines will likely do the worst job getting
you there on time. Listed here are destinations
the major airlines care so little about serving on
time that *35 percent or more* of their flights arrived at the airport *late* in 1989. This list is culled
from on-time performance statistics for 29 major
U.S. airports. Airlines are ranked worst-to-best in
order of each one's "late score"—the total number
of late percentage points above 35 percent.

Pan Am   Late score: 309

1. Chicago O'Hare (58%)
2. Salt Lake City (49%)
3. San Francisco (45%)
4. Detroit (43%)
5. Kansas City (41%)
6. Charlotte (38%)
7. Minneapolis (35%)

USAir   Late score: 296

1. Denver (56%)
2. New York JFK (48%)
3. Kansas City (42%)
4. Chicago O'Hare (39%)
5. Dallas-Ft. Worth (38%)
6. Minneapolis (38%)
7. Phoenix (35%)

Eastern Airlines   Late score: 148

1. Los Angeles (38%)
2. San Francisco (38%)
3. Chicago O'Hare (36%)
4. Phoenix (36%)

Northwest Airlines   Late score: 112

1. San Francisco (41%)
2. New York JFK (36%)
3. Las Vegas (35%)

United Airlines   Late score: 108

1. Memphis (38%)
2. Salt Lake City (35%)
3. Chicago O'Hare (35%)

TWA   Late score: 84

1. San Francisco (48%)
2. Los Angeles (36%)

Delta Air Lines   Late score: 74

1. New York JFK (38%)
2. San Francisco (36%)

continued

Continental Airlines   Late score: 35

1. NY LaGuardia (35%)

American Airlines   Late score: 0

American's worst lateness rate from among 29
major U.S. airports in 1989 was 29 percent in
Chicago. Consequently, *American does not qualify
for this poor performance list.*

Source: *Ready for Take-off Database,* USDOT.

The information contained in this box is updated regularly in *Ready for Take-off,
Database,* a quarterly publication. For subscription information, write to: *Ready for
Take-off, Database,* P.O. Box 521, Easton, PA 18044-0521.

BOX 6-3

The Airline Marketing Game: On-time Performance

Airlines just love USDOT on-time performance
statistics—especially when the numbers are in
their favor. But as with most advertising claims
about a product's or service's top rating, consumers should always be wary.

Case in point: Northwest versus American.
American advertises itself—and rightly so—as
"The On-time Machine." Still, the Machine oc-
casionally loses power. For the first few months
of 1990, American failed to earn the number-one
title among the majors, yet it continued to lay
claim to the crown by referring to the long-term
statistics rather than the short-term ones.

"For as long as the Department of Transportation has been keeping records, one airline has
done the best job of getting you where you're
going on time: American Airlines, the On-time
Machine," said a two-page ad in *Newsweek* in

June. Well, actually, America West is the *one airline* that's done the *best* job, but American surely left out the words "one *major* airline" by mistake.

Among the majors, in December 1989, Northwest won first place in on-time performance for the month and made advertising hay of the fact. In January 1990, Northwest fell to third place, beating American by a hair. In February and March, Northwest held second place, 2 to 5 points behind the leader but comfortably ahead of American. How did Northwest ads play this? Big. Playing on American's rightful reputation as number one in on-time performance, Northwest's ads trumpeted: "Once again, Northwest finished ahead of American in on-time performance . . . So why wait for American? Next time, fly Northwest."

The implication: if Northwest beat the number 1 airline, Northwest must be the new number 1. Over the short haul among the major airlines, Northwest *had* climbed to second and third place; over the long run, though, it remained a solid fifth.

Your Rights If the Flight Is Late

Under their contract of carriage with you, airlines almost always assume no consequent liability for delayed, late, or canceled flights. That means if a late plane causes you to miss a connection, which causes you to miss an important meeting or eats up one of your four vacation days, you have no legal claim against the airline under the terms of your contract. Nor do any federal regulations or state laws mandate compensation. However, that does not necessarily mean tough luck for you. Airline personnel often have some discretion to compensate you for the inconvenience—free drinks while you're waiting on the plane, reimbursement for meals or hotel during your delay, endorsement of your ticket to another airline that *can* get you to your destination more promptly.

To recoup losses under these conditions requires assertiveness and the ability to get action. Chapter 7 contains all the information you'll need to negotiate a deal.

Protecting Yourself from Late Flights

The best way to protect yourself from poor on-time performance is to never schedule split-second timing for connections or meetings. Since stagecoach days, transportation delays have been a fact of life. As air travel volume continues to grow in the United States and overseas, delays promise to be more common rather than less so. Plan accordingly.

Another important protection is to learn the recent on-time performance record for the specific flights you're planning to take. This information can be found on computerized reservations systems. To get the on-time performances record of the specific flight you're taking, ask the travel agent or airline ticket agent, or consult the OAG Electronic Edition on your computer.

Performance is rated on a scale from 0 to 9, with 0 indicating flights most likely to arrive late and 9 denoting flights most likely to arrive on time. Thus, a flight such as United's 1017 from LaGuardia to Dulles gets a "9" for its 90 to 100 percent on-time performance. USAir's flight 1170 from Charlotte-Douglas (NC) to Tampa, on time just 13 percent of the time in March 1990, earned a "1."

If your flight is canceled and you want to reschedule, you might skip the long line of angry customers at gate check-in. Go to a telephone immediately to book reservations on the next available flight whether on a different carrier or on the one that just canceled the flight. Your aim is to beat the crowd rushing to book all available seats. But be discreet. One clerk saw an astute traveler do this and had to deal with a near riot when angry line-waiters found out they'd been outmaneuvered.

If you subscribe to the OAGEE, print out a list of all the flights going to your destination on your day of departure. That way you'll know who to call in an instant.

BOX 6-4

Can You Trust the Statistics?

USDOT statistics show that the airlines' average on-time performance improved between 1987 and 1990. In December 1987, 33 percent of the major airlines' flights were late—arrived at the gate more than 15 minutes behind schedule. By March 1990, despite increased air traffic congestion and more flight departures, lateness had shrunk to 23 percent.

How did they do it? Well, instead of improving performance, the airlines simply readjusted the schedules. "Publication of the performance

continued

statistics gave carriers the incentive to artificially adjust schedules and build in delay time," explains Dan Smith, former spokesman for the 100,000-member International Airline Passengers Association.

One regular flyer noticed this on his periodic trips between Cleveland and New York. "This is supposed to a one-hour flight," he says. "Now it's scheduled for about an hour and a half."

On one American Airlines' arrivals monitor at JFK Airport in June 1989, flight 45 from Paris, scheduled to arrive at 2:55 P.M., was shown to be actually expected at 2:11 P.M. Flight 47 from Lyons was expected almost an hour ahead of its scheduled 3:25 P.M. arrival time.

It's tough to be late when you give yourself so much leeway.

This explains why you can be delayed pushing away from the gate, held on the runway, circling an airport, or stuck on the tarmac waiting for a gate to become available yet still arrive "on-time." What's important to your schedule is pinning down the airline to a realistic arrival time—regardless of whether the schedule allows for today's delays.

With all airlines playing the same scheduling game, comparisons among the airlines' performance numbers should hold true. Thus America West's, Southwest's, and American's top status should be accurate, whereas the statistic that says 21.9 percent of all airline's flights were late *on average* may be an understatement.

Of more concern is the fact that the USDOT also allows airlines to massage the numbers in their own favor—by not counting flights delayed because of what they say are "mechanical problems."

How many bad marks do the airlines remove—1

percent, 5 percent, 20 percent? "We know the number left out, but I won't say if that number is significant or insignificant," says the USDOT's Hoyte Decker. "I'm not going to say they're not cheating—that would be too sweeping. There could always be some cheating going on. But we make an effort to assure the data is accurate. I'm satisfied."

Despite the limitations, and because there is no alternative data base, the USDOT's on-time performance numbers—when viewed in proper perspective—are the best available.

TABLE 6-2

How Good Is Your Airport?

Sometimes the problem of late arrivals is caused more by the airport than by the airline. Shown below are the average percentage of flights arriving late in 1989 at each of 29 airports. The nation's largest airports are noted in parentheses next to the airport name. The absolute worst airports tend to be older giants suffering from overcapacity. More modern hulking aerodromes—like DFW, Houston Intercontinental, and Atlanta—perform much better.

Code	Airport	Percentage of Flights Arriving Late
LAS	Las Vegas McCarran International	18
DFW	Dallas-Ft. Worth (2)	19
IAH	Houston Intercontinental	19
MEM	Memphis International	19
ATL	Atlanta Hartsfield (4)	20
MSP	Minneapolis-St. Paul International	20
SLC	Salt Lake City International	20

continued

Code	Airport	Percentage of Flights Arriving Late
IAD	Washington Dulles	21
PHX	Phoenix Sky Harbor	21
STL	St. Louis Lambert Airport	21
DTW	Detroit Metropolitan Wayne Co.	22
DEN	Denver Stapleton (7)	23
MCI	Kansas City International	24
SAN	San Diego International	24
	AVERAGE	25
LAX	Los Angeles International (3)	25
MCO	Orlando International	25
TPA	Tampa International	25
DCA	Washington National	25
BOS	Boston Logan	26
PIT	Greater Pittsburgh International	26
MIA	Miami International (8)	27
SEA	Seattle-Tacoma International	27
PHL	Philadelphia International	28
EWR	Newark International	29
JFK	New York JFK International (5)	29
CLT	Charlotte-Douglas	31
LGA	New York LaGuardia (9)	32
ORD	Chicago O'Hare (1)	32
SFO	San Francisco International (6)	34

Source: USDOT.

Overbooking

You may have already heard the bit of over-booking folklore making the rounds with frequent fliers these days. According to legend, the national airline of a small third-world military dictatorship booked three times too many passengers for a flight. The solution: military personnel armed with automatic weapons lined up the would-be passengers on the sweltering runway. The passengers were then ordered to run around the parked 747 three times. The first to finish would get seats.

The rules are more civilized in America, of course. If a flight is overbooked, the airline must ask for volunteers to give up their seats. Some 655,000 travelers voluntarily gave up their seats in 1989. If there aren't enough volunteers, the airline boots people off the flight. More than 110,000 passengers were involuntarily "bumped" in 1989.

Bumping is a carryover from the days of regulated air travel, when you could book as many seats on an airplane as you wanted and then just not show up at the airport. Before APEX tickets, there was no monetary penalty for no-shows. To keep their planes full, airlines booked more passengers than they had seats for, on the assumption that a certain percentage of people would just never show up at the gate. With most tickets sold in advance, often with hefty cancellation penalties, overbooking should be a dinosaur. Airlines, however, still make use of the practice.

Despite the inconvenience and annoyance to paying customers, some airlines use overbooking more than others. Table 6-3 shows which airlines will gladly tell customers to take a hike and which treat their customers with more respect.

TABLE 6-3

Airline Bumping

Ranked worst-to-best, based on the number of ticketed passengers involuntarily denied boarding per 100,000 in 1989.

Airline	Number of Passengers Bumped per 100,000
America West	108
Presidential	107
Aloha	61
Southwest	49
Aspen	49
TWA	48
Piedmont	46
Pan Am	46
USAir	40
Northwest	38
Markair	38
Emerald	37
Continental	32
AVERAGE	30
Alaska	24
Eastern	24
Hawaiian	19
Horizon	16
Braniff	13
Midwest Express	13
Delta	11
Midway	9
United	6
Florida Express	2

continued

Airline	Number of Passengers Bumped per 100,000
Air Wisconsin	1
American	1
American Trans Air	0
Reeve	0
Tower	0

Source: USDOT.

The information contained in this table is updated regularly in *Ready for Take-off Database*, a quarterly publication. For subscription information, write to: *Ready for Take-off Database*, P.O. Box 521, Easton, PA 18044-0521.

Volunteering Your Seat

Whether you give up your seat voluntarily or are kicked off the plane, USDOT rules require that the customer receive compensation for the inconvenience or injustice. There is no set minimum amount of compensation for volunteers. You can and should bargain for the best deal possible.

Typically, airlines will offer a free ticket. But before you accept one, find out what restrictions apply to that ticket. "A number of people have been having trouble with free-ticket restrictions as to what dates and times of day they can be used," says New York State Attorney General Robert Abrams.

Before volunteering, you should find out how long you'll have to wait before you can get on another flight. Can the airline confirm you on that next flight or just get you on the waiting list? If a more convenient flight is available on another carrier, get the airline that bumped you to endorse your ticket to that airline so you don't have to pay an additional nonadvanced purchase fare. And don't forget to negotiate compensation for your added expenses should your delay be a lengthy one: hotel, meals, telephone calls to notify family and/or business that you've been delayed.

How good a compensation deal can you get if you voluntarily give up your seat? Understand that if you want cash, the compensation that airlines must pay to involuntarily bumped passengers according to law (explained later) will likely be your bargaining ceiling. That's because if there aren't enough volunteers, the airline will do the choosing for you. A free ticket, on the other hand, which costs the airline little, could be worth a bundle to you.

While negotiations and settlements with volunteers vary from airline to airline and incident to incident, we've developed an index that rates how attractive the offers for volunteers are, based on the ratio of voluntary to involuntary bumpings in 1989. An airline that has a lot of people voluntarily giving up their seats must be making offers the passengers can't refuse. Thus, the higher the index number shown on Table 6-4, the better the deal.

TABLE 6-4

Does it Pay to Volunteer?

Airlines ranked best-to-worst on how good a deal they strike with customers who voluntarily give up their seats when a flight is overbooked. The attractiveness index is based on the ratio of passengers who voluntarily surrendered their seat (presumably for attractive compensation) to those who were involuntarily bumped from a flight in 1989.

continued

Airline	Attractiveness of Giving Up Your Seat (index)
American	209.6
Florida Express	97.5
Air Wisconsin	41.4
United	39.3
Midway	31.0
AVERAGE	**19.7**
Delta	9.0
Alaska	8.0
Braniff	7.7
Eastern	7.4
Aspen	5.3
USAir	5.0
Northwest	4.3
Piedmont	4.0
Continental	3.9
Midwest Express	3.8
Markair	3.0
Pan Am	2.9
Presidential	2.6
Southwest	2.3
Horizon	2.2
TWA	1.9
America West	1.3
Hawaiian	0.1
Aloha	0.02
Emerald	0.0
American Trans Air	NA
Reeve	NA
Tower	NA

Source: USDOT.

The information contained in this table is updated regularly in *Ready for Take-off Database*, a quarterly publication. For subscription information, write to: *Ready for Take-off Database*, P.O. Box 521, Easton, PA 18044-0521.

Here again, American outclassed everyone else. More than 111,000 passengers apparently found the terms of voluntarily giving up their seat very attractive at American. Just 533 passengers out of more than 72 million had to be forced off American Airlines flights in 1989. That resulted in an attractiveness index rating of 209.6—well above every other airline. That pulled up the average, making all other major airlines except United below average performers in this area. Once again, with passenger cooperation like that, American *knows* how to treat its customers.

Hawaiian, Aloha, and Emerald were at the other end of the spectrum. Out of 919 overbooked passengers on Hawaiian, only 51 voluntarily gave up seats. Of the 2,473 too many passengers at Aloha, only 49 volunteered to give up their seat. On Emerald, no passengers would volunteer so 9 had to be bumped. American Trans Air, Reeve, and Tower had no overbookings and thus bumped no passengers.

Your Rights if Involuntarily Bumped

Under USDOT rules, passengers bumped against their will must be paid an amount equal to the one-way fare to their final destination, up to a $200 maximum. That's if the carrier arranges substitute transportation scheduled to get you to your destination no more than 2 hours after your original arrival time. If the alternative flight gets you there more than 2 hours later, you should be paid *twice* the one-way fare, to a maximum of $400. (Of course, you keep your original ticket and can use it on another flight without penalty.)

Sound complicated? It is. And that's only the tip of the iceberg; there are numerous conditions and limitations. Refer to Box 6-5 for an easy-to-understand translation of USDOT bureaucratese into English.

Instead of cash, the airline may offer to compensate you with a free ticket. As with voluntary deals, watch out for ticket restrictions and carefully weigh the potential value of the ticket. You can always demand the cash.

If you believe the compensation insufficiently covers your losses, don't cash the airline's compensation check or use the free ticket! That could be legally construed as settlement in full.

Using the action techniques described in Chapter 7, take your case to corporate headquarters. If you still can't get what you believe you're due, you can sue the airline. But, before you ever go to court, be dead certain you have a realistic case, real losses, and proof of those losses.

BOX 6-5

Do You Qualify for Bumping Compensation?

If you are bumped from a flight involuntarily, the airline may have to compensate you. But there are loopholes and fine print galore. Here's how to tell what you're entitled to under the airline contract of carriage and USDOT regulations.

1. Did you have a confirmed reservation and did you meet the airline's deadline for purchase of the ticket?

continued

2. Did you check in at the airport, ticket counter, or gate according to the airline's check-in deadlines?

3. Did the plane you were scheduled to fly on have more than 60 seats?

If you answered yes to *all* of these questions, proceed to #4. If you answered no to *any one* of these questions, the airline is not required to compensate you.

4. Were you bumped because the airline substituted a *smaller* plane than the one originally scheduled for the flight?

5. Were you bumped from a charter flight?

6. Were you bumped from a flight *originating outside* the United States?

7. Were you denied boarding because the flight was canceled?

8. Were you denied boarding because of conditions beyond the airline's control or because of a government requisition of space on the plane?

9. Were you denied boarding because you:

   a. refused to permit a search of your person for weapons, explosives, or drugs;

   b. refused to produce positive identification on request;

   c. were disorderly, abusive, or violent;

   d. appeared to be intoxicated or under the influence of drugs;

   e. attempted to interfere with any member of the flight crew;

   f. appeared to be mentally deranged or incapacitated;

   g. refused to obey instructions from the flight crew;

   h. had a contagious disease or offensive odor;

    i. were dressed in a manner that would cause discomfort or offense to other passengers;

    j. were barefoot;

    k. did anything that might jeopardize the safety of the aircraft or its occupants;

    l. had a mental or physical condition such that you would require assistance in an emergency or care of your physical needs in flight *and you are not accompanied by a competent attendant* who is responsible for caring for you in-flight;

and did the contract of carriage give the airline the right to refuse to board you under any of these circumstances?

If you answered yes to *any one* of these questions, the airline is not required to compensate you. If you answered no to *all* of these questions, proceed to #10.

  10. Did the airline arrange for *any* substitute transportation to get you to your destination?

If yes, proceed to #11. If no, you are entitled to *double your one-way airfare* up to a maximum amount of $400. Thus, if your one-way fare were $250 × 2 = $500, the airline would only have to pay $400. But if your one-way fare were $130 × 2 = $260, you'd be entitled to $260.

  11. Did the airline arrange substitute transportation that is *scheduled* to get you to your destination *within 1 hour* of the scheduled arrival time of your original flight?

If you answered yes, the airline owes you nothing. If the answer is no, proceed to #12.

  12. Was the flight you were bumped from (originating in the United States) bound for a *domestic* or *international* destination?

If you answered "international," jump ahead to #14. If you answered "domestic," see #13.

continued

Domestic Flights

13. Did the airline arrange substitute transportation that was scheduled to get you to your destination *less than* 2 hours later or *more than* 2 hours later than your originally scheduled flight?

If "less than 2 hours later," the airline must pay you an amount equal to the one-way fare to your final destination. However, there is a $200 ceiling on that payment.

If "more than 2 hours later," the airline must pay you an amount equal to *double* the one-way fare to your final destination, up to a maximum penalty of $400.

International Flights

14. Did the airline arrange substitute transportation that was scheduled to get you to your destination *less than* 4 hours later or *more than* 4 hours later than your originally scheduled flight?

If "less than 4 hours later," the airline must pay you an amount equal to the one-way fare to your final destination. However, there is a $200 ceiling on that payment.

If "more than 4 hours later," the airline must pay you an amount equal to *double* the one-way fare to your final destination, up to a maximum penalty of $400.

Protect Yourself from Bumping

To reduce your chances of being bumped, ask an airline representative what the check-in and reconfirmation rules of the airline are when you buy your ticket, *and* consult the airline's contract of carriage. As Table 6-5 shows, check-in times can vary widely, especially for international flights.

TABLE 6-5

Check-in Time

Airline check-in times ranked best-to-worst based on the shortest amount of time before domestic flight departure that a passenger can check in without having his ticket canceled. Where domestic check-in times are the same, airlines are ranked first according to their international check-in requirements, then alphabetically.

Airline	Check-in Time Before Departure (minutes)	
	Domestic	International
United	10 G	20 Ga
		30 Gb
Eastern	10 G	30 G
USAir	10 G	30 G
Delta	10 G	30 Ac
		45 Ad
Northwest	10 G	30 Ge
		60 Gf
American	15 G	20 G
Continental	15 G	30 G
TWA	30 A	90 A
Pan Am	60 A	120 A

Source: Airline information.

G = Gate
A = Airport check-in counter
a = for flights to the Bahamas, Canada, and Mexico
b = for all international flights except those covered by footnote "a"
c = international, nontransatlantic flights
d = transatlantic flights
e = for flights to Canada, Mexico, and the Caribbean
f = for all international flights except those covered by footnote "e"

For domestic flights, most airlines require check-in 10 minutes before departure; American, TWA, Continental, and Pan Am require more time—15 to 60 minutes.

On international flights, check-in times range from United's 20 minutes, to the more typical 30 minutes before departure, to TWA's and Pan Am's huge 90- and 120-minute, respective, requirements.

To speed you through the airport and on to the boarding gate, get your boarding pass and seat assignment when you buy your tickets, if that's possible. To avoid a holdup at a baggage-check counter, check your luggage with streetside baggage-check personnel at the terminal entrance, if the airline offers that service.

Try not to cut your check-in time too close to the airline's minimum requirements. Arrive at the airport and check in early— at least 1 hour before departure for domestic flights and 2 hours before international flights. Most airlines will bump the latest arrivers first, but keep in mind that low-fare customers can be very attractive candidates for bumping instead.

Bungled Baggage

There are perhaps few things more frustrating than lost, damaged, pilfered, or late luggage. If you fly with any frequency, sooner or later, you will have a story to tell.

Getting your luggage to your destination and back into your hands seems like an easy enough job for an airline, yet some carriers find it a much more insurmountable task than others. Table 6-6 ranks the airlines on the number of mishandled bags per 100,000 passengers in 1989. Southwest does the best job by far of any major airline. Its

TABLE 6-6

Baggage Handlers and Mishandlers

Airlines ranked best-to-worst based on how many bags per 100,000 passengers were mishandled—lost, damaged, pilfered, delayed—in 1989. These numbers are for domestic airline baggage mishandling, and do not include baggage problems on international flights.

Airline	Mishandled Baggage Reports per 100,000 Passengers	Domestic Passengers Boarded	Net Numbers of Mishandled Baggage Reports
Southwest	376	20,240,845	76,088
Pan Am	596	8,545,755	50,924
Continental	661	34,313,910	226,806
United	704	54,294,869	382,064
Delta	708	65,400,755	462,837
Alaska Airlines	721	5,095,813	36,757
American	731	69,597,348	508,430
America West	732	13,300,447	97,309
Northwest	761	34,247,469	260,728
AVERAGE	767		
TWA	883	22,334,219	197,275
USAir/Piedmont	974	63,620,435	619,713
Eastern	1,257	13,293,684	167,042

Source: USDOT.

The information contained in this table is updated regularly in *Ready for Take-off Database*, a quarterly publication. For subscription information, write to: *Ready for Take-off Database*, P.O. Box 521, Easton, PA 18044-0521.

rate of mishandling is just 376 per 100,000 passengers—less than half the industry average. Most of the others mishandle at a rate of between 600 and 760 bags per 100,000 passengers. The worst baggage handlers by a significant margin are those at Eastern and USAir, screwing up 1,257 and 974 bags, respectively, per 100,000 passengers. Eastern's rate is high: roughly one passenger on every departure has a problem on average versus one person for every two flights at most other airlines. Southwest has to fly four planeloads of people before it fouls up one person's bags.

You can increase your odds of avoiding trouble by taking precautions seasoned travelers have long known about. If you're going on a short trip of a day or two, pack one bag and carry it onto the plane. Use a soft bag rather than a rigid case; it's easier to mold to the dimensions of underseat or overhead storage spaces.

If you have to turn your luggage over to baggage handlers, use convenient curbside check-in, if the airline offers it. Wherever you check in, "Watch the tag go on each bag to make sure it's going to your final destination. Sometimes the clerk will mistakenly tag it to the connecting city instead of your ultimate destination," says Marge Conway, director of the Executive Travel Management Service at American Express Travel Related Services. Check that the coded destination and flight number on your baggage stub match those on your ticket. Of course, remove any old baggage stubs from previous trips.

The fewer connections, the fewer chances the

airline has to screw up. Although connections are increasingly common in today's hub-city airline system, fly direct if possible.

The worst time of year for mishandled baggage, as Table 6-7 shows, is December, when everybody wants to fly through the same narrow holiday window. In December 1988, and December 1989, the major airlines mishandled an average 1,068 pieces of luggage per 100,000 passengers—42 percent above the average foul-up rate. So if you're traveling by air in December, be espe-

TABLE 6-7

When Do Airlines Bobble Baggage Most?

Average mishandled baggage rates of the major airlines month by month based on 1988 and 1989 data.

Month	Average Number of Mishandled Baggage Reports per 100,000 Passengers	Number of Passengers Boarded
January	985	29,914,946
February	806	29,769,797
March	751	35,955,834
April	634	33,219,674
May	609	34,524,690
June	696	36,075,090
July	725	36,576,510
August	761	38,636,672
September	648	31,617,114
October	654	34,541,072
November	658	33,175,611
December	1,068	32,656,102
AVERAGE	750	

Source: USDOT.

cially careful to take precautions against baggage problems. During the peak air travel season—June, July, and August—baggage mishaps run about average. They are slightly lower than average in spring and fall.

Another important step, just in case: don't pack expensive valuables in your luggage—jewelry, laptop computers, cameras, eyeglasses, fax machines, irreplaceable items, rare antique vases, securities, and especially not cash—unless the airline's contract will accept liability for loss of such items. Some airline contracts of carriage, such as American's, Northwest's, and TWA's, state that the airline is *not* liable for such items when checked as baggage—*even if excess valuation is declared*. If that's the case, stow these items in your carry-on bags; keep them with you and keep an eye on them, because some airlines refuse to assume liability for such items, even in the passenger compartment.

Other airlines, like Delta, Eastern, and USAir, will assume liability for losses on certain valuables in your baggage, but you have to declare the excess valuation and buy additional baggage insurance coverage. This usually costs a couple of dollars per extra $100 of value. Excess valuation protection might be well worth the price. Industry sources say luggage covered by the insurance gets more personal treatment.

If you purchase an expensive item on your journey and are planning to check it as baggage, consider having the item shipped home via a parcel delivery service—and insure it for its full value.

If the worst does happen, be ready to go to bat to get compensation. Report damages, delayed and lost bags, or thefts as soon as you discover them. The airline will have forms for you to fill out before it even starts bargaining with you for repayment; for late bags, airline personnel at the airport may give you some advance money to cover your immediate needs.

The most persnickety requirement of the whole procedure is proof of your loss. Yes, if your bag never showed up, it's clearly lost. But how does the airline know you really had a $500 Halston dress or an $800 Armani suit in there? And did you *really* spend $700 for the luggage itself? As you might expect, the airline will demand receipts, and hopefully you've retained these at home. But be forewarned: if you bought the suitcase four years ago or the suit two years ago, the airline will only want to pay the *depreciated* value of the items, not the full replacement value. Depreciated value is, of course, lower than replacement value (and used clothing depreciates very rapidly) because you've used up part of the value of the lost suit or suitcase.

To protect your investments, we recommend this: if you're going to be making new clothes purchases for your trip, make them when you reach your destination—and retain all receipts. That way there's less to carry on your outbound journey (and less for the airline to lose) and, more important, your new purchases will have depreciated little because you've just bought them *and may never have worn them yet*. Shopping in

CHAPTER 7

How to Get Action, Where to Complain

You've just survived flying on Hell Airlines.

The odyssey began when you saw HA's advertised super-low fares. Yet somehow the fare was not available for any of two dozen dates you tried. You settled on a fare $250 higher. At the airport, long lines at HA's baggage-check counter caused you to almost miss your flight. When you got to the gate, you learned the airline overbooked the flight and "bumped" you—refused to let you board the plane for lack of seats—even though you paid for your tickets a month ago.

Your later flight's takeoff was delayed 3 hours for some never-explained reason. You finally landed in Seattle with two blown landing gear tires; your luggage landed at approximately the same time—in Cleveland. The flight attendant, surly for most of the trip, *was* pleasant as you departed: "Thank you for flying Hell Airlines. When you travel in the future and want to know where to go for air service, remember our motto— " 'Go to Hell!' "

That, however, won't be possible. Halfway through your vacation, HA filed for bankruptcy and discontinued service, stranding you without a return flight. Want a refund? Line up behind 50,000 other unsecured creditors.

You Can *Solve Air Travel Problems*

If you follow the advice in this book, you should be able to avoid the Hell Airlines experience. Despite even the most careful planning, however, things can and *do* go wrong. Airlines with a good baggage-handling record still lose some luggage; airlines with the lowest number of complaints filed against them still rub some people the wrong way; air carriers with an excellent safety record still suffer crashes. It could happen to you.

When you incur frustrations and/or damages because of an airline, in most cases you can get the problem repaired—if you know how to get action.

Most consumer advocates tell you to complain. We disagree. You don't want to complain, you want *action*. You get action by making airline personnel aware of your problem, developing one or several solutions, then convincing the airline people to carry out the solution. That's significantly different than complaining. Getting action requires your involvement with airline personnel— a partnership of equals—to solve a specific problem. Of necessity, you must possess negotiating skills and a knowledge of possible solutions.

Complaining, on the other hand, immediately puts you in a subordinate position (like a child) and causes you to abdicate the true command position of the consumer. Children complain because they have no authority to act, they often lack the experience and intelligence to find their own solution to the problem, and they don't know how to negotiate a deal that meets the needs of both adult and child. Adult complaining is a more sophisticated version of a child's whining. The goal is to annoy the other party to the point that they do what you want just to shut you up.

You don't want to be a baby. That's physiologically and emotionally stressful for you. Worse, it's usually frustratingly ineffective.

Here are the nuts-and-bolts details on how to get action.

Know What You Want

One of the biggest impediments to successful negotiating is to lack a clear sense of exactly what you want from the other party. You already know how the airline has harmed you; now, what would be a satisfactory solution to the problem?

If you just complain about your problem to a gate clerk or ticket agent, you're leaving the difficult task of problem solving up to someone who is probably not trained to be a troubleshooter. It's no wonder that you get an answer like, "There's nothing I can do."

No one knows your needs better than you do, so it's up to you to develop a solution. Figure out a range of possible remedies before you approach anyone with your problem.

In developing your solutions, be creative. Suppose your direct flight from New York to Chicago has been canceled. The solution that comes to mind first is to demand a seat on the next available direct flight on that airline. But that flight might not depart for another 2 hours and no seats may be available. Consider other negotiable options. You could suggest being rerouted to your destination via a connecting flight through, say, Detroit, which might leave earlier than the next available direct flight.

Another possibility: tell the gate agent to endorse your ticket to another airline, which may have available seating on a flight boarding right now. Because last-minute ticket purchases are expensive compared to APEX fares, make sure the airline that canceled your original flight will make up the difference between the lower fare you paid for its ticket and the higher price of the new ticket you now have to purchase.

If there is no flight out until the next day, negotiate for compensation for your added expenses due to the delay—hotel, meals, phone calls.

Know What to Expect

Obviously, the solution you come up with must be reasonable. No matter how much you've been annoyed and inconvenienced by the flight attendant who accidentally spilled a cup of coffee on your suit, you're not going to get a $20,000 court judgment against the airline. Expect compensation for the cost of the damages—having the suit cleaned and maybe free use of employee facilities where you can clean up at the destination airport. Sharp negotiators may also be able to bargain for something extra, the equivalent of compensation for pain and suffering so the airline can regain your goodwill—a $25 coupon toward your next flight, perhaps, or an in-flight upgrade to first class.

Beyond realistic expectations, compensation for some common hassles is regulated by government rules and international treaties. For example, if you're involuntarily bumped from a flight, the U.S. Department of Transportation requires that the airline pay you one of two maximum penalties ($200 or $400), subject to several specific criteria. (For complete details on compensation rules related to the major hassles, see Chapter 6.)

Compensation for the death of a passenger on international flights is limited to $75,000 by the Warsaw Convention, unless you can prove willful misconduct on the part of the airline.

Understand the Written and Unwritten Contracts

Your airline travel is also governed by a written contract between you and the airline. The terms of agreement are specifically spelled out in a contract called the Conditions of Carriage. This contract is often printed on the back of your ticket in abbreviated form. A more detailed version must be provided by the airline by law, if you ask for it. The airline must make this contract available to you for viewing at its ticket office; you can also get your own copy by writing the airline.

As you might expect, this contract contains numerous technical loopholes airlines can wriggle through to avoid complying with the implicit agreement. Don't let the letter of the contract limit your getting action on the spirit of the contract. For beyond the written contract—and airline attorneys will deny this—every airline *must* accept the terms of an unwritten contract with the public. An airline like Northwest, which represents itself as an on-time flier, should get you there on time. Airlines like American, Delta, and United, which point to their high customer satisfaction ratings, top-quality service, or special attention, had better deliver. Legal mumbo-jumbo in the contract of carriage notwithstanding, any airline that consistently fails to live up to the agreement it makes with customers through its advertising and public relations image will soon find customers refusing to renew the contract for their *next* flight. Taking your business elsewhere is the consumer's ultimate weapon.

Talk to the Right Authorities

Armed with the knowledge of what you want and the outside limits of what you can expect, you're ready to approach someone to get action. Start with airline personnel. Most airlines have a customer service representative at the airport who can write checks on the spot for denied boarding compensation, give stranded passengers money for extra expenses due to delays or cancellations (within limits), endorse his or her airline's tickets to another airline, and settle other common problems. Often you can get a solution right then and there.

One passenger on a Delta flight delayed almost an hour in New York because of mechanical difficulties got help by lassoing a stewardess. He got right to the point and explained clearly and concisely that he was traveling to officiate at the funeral of a close friend. Because of the delay, he might not make his connecting flight in Atlanta and risked missing the funeral. The stewardess talked to the flight crew and they worked out a solution that made up for the delay. In Atlanta, the passenger was met on the tarmac by a Delta employee with a car. The car rushed the passenger to the distant gate of his connecting flight to Augusta and he made it to the funeral on time.

Try to determine what authority the person you're talking to has to provide a solution. If that person doesn't have clout, move up the ladder to higher airline officials. Frequently, underlings won't come right out and admit they have no authority. That means you've got to decode key put-off phrases that signal lack of authority: "There's nothing I can do," "That's not airline policy," "That's not allowed," or "The only thing I can do for you is X or Y." Another tipoff is when your conversation—or argument—begins going in circles. When the lower-level employee thus tells you you've reached the limit of your options (and none of the options matches *your* solution), it's time to call in the higher-ups.

Another reason you should appeal to a higher authority is the possibility that the person you're dealing with simply doesn't know the rules. This is sometimes the case with child safety seats. Boarding-gate personnel may forbid you to use your child's safety seat on the grounds that it isn't approved by the FAA for use on aircraft. The seat may not state in writing that it meets FAA standards, but any seat manufactured after 1985 that lives up to auto-safety standards is approved by the FAA. Not all airline personnel know this, which means you have to find a superior who *is* familiar with the rules.

Tip Your Hat to Supervisors

A strategy point: although it is frustrating to deal with a low-level employee who can't help you or doesn't know how, do not transfer any anger that has built up against that person to the supervisor. Workers are not trained to rethink company policy, they're taught to carry out specifically defined tasks.

Managers, conversely, are problem solvers. They have a broader perspective on the ins and outs of company rules. They more fully understand the corporate value of good customer relations. They have a bigger career stake in solving your problem because they're at least partly responsible for smooth and efficient operation within their realm. They have authority to make adjustments.

It is therefore in your best interest to make this person your *friend*. Make your anger disappear and be pleasant whenever it's time to talk to the next level of authority. Calmly let the supervisor know what the problem is, how you've been harmed, and what the solution is. Explain that you know your problem is unfortunately beyond the capabilities of the person you've been trying to work with. Indicate that you are already relieved upon the manager's arrival. Why? Because you have full confidence the supervisor is more than qualified to solve this problem.

Keep Emotions in Check

Because the squeaky wheel gets the grease, there are some instances in which an angry or emotionally upset customer may intimidate airline personnel into action. Rarely will you get action on the strength of your bluster alone. We advise *against* explosive anger.

People who deal with the public learn to identify and resist troublemakers. No matter how unhelpful, obstructive, or just plain stupid an airline employee may be, avoid the temptation to get emotional, lest you be improperly tagged a crackpot. Belligerent bellyaching erodes your bargaining position by diverting attention away from the issue and toward your behavior as a seeming troublemaker. People who rant and rave lack credibility. Managers deal with quarrelsome gadflys all the time, and they're an instant turnoff. You don't want to be mistaken for one of them, so remain calm and don't let the situation get your goat.

Sometimes, however, despite your reasonable demands, you will be erroneously portrayed as a troublemaker. Recognize this as a negotiating maneuver designed to make you feel unjustified in your claims. If you believe attention is being incorrectly diverted to your conduct, make the truth of the situation crystal clear: there is a problem—

which already exists, and will not disappear without a solution—and there is you, whose job it is to enforce a solution. You want to help the manager solve what is now *his* problem caused by his airline.

There is another good reason not to let anger and tactics of intimidation spin out of control, especially when you're aboard the plane: you could get arrested. Federal law prohibits anyone from interfering with or jeopardizing the safety of the aircraft, its passengers, or flight personnel. A raving lunatic hurling threats and abuse clearly fits the bill. Throw a punch, and there are federal marshals in your future.

On the ground, airlines can refuse to transport you if you are abusive or disorderly. Obviously, if you are violent or threaten airline personnel—whether you've been provoked or not—you could be subject to arrest and legal action.

Of course, you want none of that. Stay calm. If you've attempted but failed to get action on the spot, there are other more sensible ways to get action.

Be Businesslike

Behaving calmly does not mean acting meek or humble. Your stance should be professional, businesslike.

That requires that you speak sensibly and clearly. Let the other person have his turn to speak. If you don't understand, ask for clarification. If you don't seem to be getting your point across, seek out the cause of the apparent miscommunication by asking questions.

Think like the kind of businessperson adept at getting *around* obstacles rather than going through them. For example, suppose a boarding attendant informs you that your briefcase, garment bag, and pocketbook put you over the limit of two carry-on items per passenger. You could light into the problem head-on and try to convince the attendant to make an exception, call in the supervisors, and hold up the flight. Or you could stash the pocketbook inside the garment bag and reduce your three items to two. Another way around the wall instead of through it: ask another passenger with one or no carry-on items to carry one of yours onto the plane.

It's a good idea to carry a small notebook to write down what was said when a problem arises. Take everyone's name. A written record provides two benefits. If the other person backtracks or denies having said something, your notes should settle the dispute. Also, being "on the record" *by name* can be intimidating to some people and may make them act more responsibly in dealing with you.

Do your homework, too. Nothing undercuts your bargaining position more than not having your facts straight or making careless accusations. That hurt one passenger annoyed at being delayed more than an hour in Detroit.

The scheduled Northwest Airlines pilot for the Detroit-Atlanta flight was delayed on his way from Milwaukee, so Northwest called in a replacement pilot, who lived 50 miles from the airport. By the time that pilot arrived, one frustrated passenger made remarks (apparently without a shred of evidence) that the replacement pilot had probably been partying. (A month earlier, three Northwest Airlines pilots *were* arrested and accused of flying while intoxicated. Subsequent blood tests showed alcohol levels above federal limits.)

The pilot in Detroit heard the false accusation and insisted on being tested for blood alcohol levels. These tests later found *no* alcohol in the pilot's system, but because the results were not available immediately, yet another pilot had to be called in. The flight finally departed 4 hours behind schedule—without the complaining passenger, who had become the target of other passengers' verbal abuse.

Assume a Firm and Knowledgeable Stance

Do not fail to let whomever you're negotiating with know *you* know your stuff. Exhibit a familiarity with the contract of carriage, general knowledge of the airline's policies, an understanding of government rules that protect you, and good old-fashioned consumer savvy.

Explain that you want to cooperate as much as possible with the airline's attempt to solve this problem, but remind them that you know where to take the battle if the matter is not resolved to your satisfaction. For example, if you're the victim of a misleading airline advertisement, you should know you can bring the matter to your state attorney general or consumer affairs office and should be ready to use this fact as leverage.

Speak about your determination to see this matter resolved properly, your intent to involve higher authorities and/or the courts if necessary, and your willingness to report obstructive, uncooperative, and rude personnel to superiors.

Understand Negotiating Strategies

The art of negotiation is as old as the hills, so negotiating strategies have become highly developed. Some tactics, like asking what's the least you'd settle for as compensation, or asking *you* to make the first offer then trying to bargain down from there, represent fair gamesmanship. Others, like the good cop/bad cop game in which a supervisor—the good cop—would give you what you want if only *his* boss—the bad cop would let him, are less scrupulous.

You should be aware of negotiating styles so you can use those to your advantage and protect yourself from those you abhor. While anyone can learn any negotiating strategy, Gerard Nierenberg, author of *The Art of Negotiating,* and Herb Cohen, author of *You Can Negotiate Anything,* suggests you never adopt a style that runs counter to your beliefs or life philosophies. If lying is anathema to you, do not mislead the other party.

"Most people negotiate badly," says Cohen, a Chicago lawyer who helped advise former President Reagan on how to deal with the Soviets during the 1985 U.S./USSR summit in Geneva. "Most of us are raised with the erroneous mindset that if someone wins, the other guy has to lose."

Consequently, a lot of people think they must win by intimidating, insulting, and degrading the other party or by scheming and trickery. Cohen advocates the so-called win-win style. Win-win negotiation aims to reach agreement by getting below the superficial points of contention and dealing with underlying needs. By getting at those underlying drives, the real differences can be dealt with, both parties' needs can be met partially or totally, and both parties can walk away with a deal they've "won."

Choose Your Weapon

If you have tried getting action on the spot and have not succeeded, know when to give up the battle—for the moment. Assuming you're justified in your demands and you believe you are right, you must call in help.

There are plenty of places to go for help. Sometimes just mentioning you'll be contacting these parties can get on-the-spot action.

The airline's president, chief executive officer (CEO), or chairman of the board. Here's where to report unhelpful, rude employees and managers; lobby for changes in corporate policy; demand refunds or compensation for your losses; send court summonses; and report poor service by the major airline's code-sharing commuter line partners. Your letter will likely be referred to a vice president or corporate consumer affairs office, but it can't hurt to start at the top.

When writing or phoning airline top brass, follow the same principles mentioned earlier pertaining to in-person negotiating. Letters should be typed. Keep it short, businesslike, and to the point. Include photocopies of any pertinent records, tickets, evidence, but retain the originals for your own files. Copies of your letter should not be sent to everyone and anyone; choose appropriate parties who will be the greatest threat to the airline.

Be sure to include information about how much business you bring to the airline—if you're a frequent flier, for example—and any information about recommendations or warnings you intend to make about the airline to friends, business associates, or your company's travel department.

An important caution: don't exaggerate and *never make false accusations* about employees or the airline; once an untruth is in writing it is legally published and constitutes libel. You could expose yourself to a lawsuit by the libeled person or company, especially if the libeled party is harmed in any way, such as being fired. Stick to the facts only.

If you get no response, write a follow-up letter that explains where you will go for assistance next if your second letter gets no response.

In Appendix A are addresses and phone numbers of major U.S. airlines, their code-sharing partners, and remaining members of the 50 largest U.S. commuter airlines. This list covers airlines carrying more than 95 percent of all passengers.

State consumer protection offices/attorney general/ ombudsman. Contact the state offices listed in Appendix B for assistance if the airline won't cooperate; if you believe federal or state law has been violated; if you are victimized by mislead-

ing or false airline advertising or grossly "unavailable" advertised low fares.

Telephone first to find the name of the cur-
rent director, acting director, chief counsel, or
other appropriate officer and then direct your
correspondence to that person. Contact your own
state's consumer protection/attorney general's office and the state in which the airline has its
headquarters. Toll-free 800 numbers listed are
generally available only for in-state calls. Check
local phone books for county and city consumer
protection agencies, district attorney, or ombudsman who might also help you.

The Better Business Bureau. Better Business
Bureaus are nonprofit organizations sponsored
by local businesses and will mediate your problem with any business, including airlines. There
are more than 170 BBBs coast to coast, and generally the BBB you contact for help is the one
nearest the airline's headquarters. Thus, the Chicago BBB is where you go for problems with
United Airlines, whereas the Dallas BBB will
mediate American Airlines disputes.

Listed in Appendix C are the phone numbers
for BBBs in the home cities of the largest airlines. For other airlines, ask the carrier's ticket
agent in what city the airline's headquarters is
located, or refer to the listing of airline addresses
in Appendix A. Then contact the BBB national
headquarters (703-276-0100) in Arlington, Vir-
ginia, to find the number of the appropriate BBB
to contact.

Government, consumer and professional overseers.
Don't expect action from airline overseers. Seek-
ing help at the Consumer Affairs Office of the
U.S. Department of Transportation is a crapshoot;
maybe your complaint will get action, maybe it
won't. A GAO study of USDOT consumer affairs
found that the office wasn't doing all it could to
help consumers. Professional groups may have
more clout keeping members in line with association policies, and it's worth writing if you have a
complaint about one of the group's members. Un-
derstaffed consumer organizations usually won't
intervene in your case.

Nevertheless, it's worth reporting your problems to any and all of these overseers. Report to
the federal government primarily for the record,
because USDOT officials are under the impression
that consumers are generally satisfied with the
present state of air travel. Reason: only a fraction of consumers with airline problems actually
take the trouble to report to USDOT.

Peter Sontag, chairman of USTravel Systems
Inc., the third largest travel distribution company in the United States, advises consumers to
be persistent, because the USDOT is not consumer friendly. "I tried to [make a complaint to
the USDOT] this morning and was transferred
six times until I . . . was told that none of the
consumer analysts was available and that someone would get back to me," says Sontag. "If the
flying public is not deliriously happy about air
travel, the problem is that there is no clear-cut,
simple and expedient avenue to voice a complaint."
Reporting problems to consumer groups and

professional associations is worthwhile for the potential effect on big-picture issues. If a consumer group is flooded with letters about nonavailability of advertised airfares, that issue will likely find its way onto the group's agenda. A listing of these organizations can be found in Appendix D.

The press. The press can help you in two ways. First, many newspapers and news radio and TV stations have consumer hotlines or complaint departments that will sometimes intercede to settle your dispute. The most sophisticated of these is WCBS Radio's Call for Action hotline in New York (212-265-8880, Monday to Friday 11 A.M. to 1 P.M.). Call for Action will work on your problem whether or not it leads to an on-air story. TV action reporters, on the other hand, tend to sift through their mail for the most visual cases.

The second way the press can help is by reporting on a common problem. Few consumers realize it, but their letters can help set the media's agenda of coverage. If many people report the same kind of problem (e.g., late planes), that may spark an editor to assign a story. Sometimes just a single compelling letter will cause an editor or reporter to jump on a story. It is also possible a reporter is already working on a story similar to yours or has had an idea about doing such an article. Your letter could crystallize the story.

But remember, the press is interested in covering news that affects *many* people, not in reporting about one man's or woman's airline headache. So you'll have the best chance of getting coverage if your bad experience is part of a big-picture story affecting many readers or viewers. No one will run a front-page headline about how your luggage was damaged, but if you know a number of people whose luggage was damaged by the same airline or airport serving your area, maybe there's a newsworthy problem with that airline's or airport's baggage-handling practices.

Other things reporters look for in deciding if a story is worth covering:

1. Inside information. Do you know about behind-the-scenes practices that harm consumers?
2. The latest twist. Have you discovered a new way that airlines cheat the public?
3. Anecdotes. Reporters are always on the lookout for real stories to illustrate their articles.

Check local newspapers and news radio and TV stations to see if there is any interest in your kind of story. Provide the facts of your story and do some preliminary research—how many more planes were late at your airport last month versus the same month a year or two earlier? For TV, think about and point out interesting visual elements. Be sure to include a daytime and evening phone number where you can be reached if the reporter wants to pursue more facts about your story. Because of the heavy volume of mail received by the press, however, assume you *won't* get a reply.

Listed in Appendix E are several national media outlets that report on consumer air travel topics. *Ready for Take-off* is the only one that explicitly solicits tales about your airline problems, solutions, and *positive* experiences for possible inclusion in future editions. If you wish, put us on your list of organizations to receive photocopies as well. Insight, comments, and inside information about the airline business that you think other passengers will benefit from are also welcome.

Legal action.   After you've tried all other avenues and the problem still hasn't been resolved to your satisfaction, your final step is to take legal action.

That doesn't always mean incurring the expense of hiring a lawyer. For small damages, the state-operated small-claims court system is relatively simple and inexpensive. Although damage limitations vary, generally you can file a small-claims court case for losses under $1,000.

Don't be fooled by the casual, friendly nature of small-claims court. You must produce evidence—photographs, the damaged article, witnesses, receipts detailing extra expenses incurred because of the airline. You must know the laws that apply to your case; don't rely on the argument that "the airline should compensate me because that's the right thing to do." And you must also be able to point to specific contract violations, if that's what your case hinges on.

For larger losses, you can hire an attorney to advise you and press the case. Chances are you'll never see a courtroom. The airline may settle or negotiate the case with your attorney; sometimes a single letter from an attorney stating his or her intention to litigate will cause an airline's nervous legal department to settle right off the bat.

Whenever you claim a loss, however, have evidence of a genuine loss. If you missed closing a $10,000 deal because the plane was late, but closed the deal the next day anyway, where's the loss?

Finally, chances are you will never need an attorney to seek recovery for injuries or death caused by an airline. But if you do, you want a top attorney experienced in the field of aviation litigation. Don't let an attorney chase your ambulance; *you* should seek out and find *him* or *her*. Listed in Appendix F are the names and numbers of eight top aviation attorneys that aviation attorneys themselves said they'd use.

Don't underestimate the value of a human life or injury by accepting a seemingly huge payment offer from the airline soon after the accident. Quick settlement offers usually are significantly smaller than the amount you could win in court. Although most settlements are sealed from public view, airlines may compensate victims or their families with a wide range of amounts, from several hundred thousand dollars to several million.

"We have won jury verdicts of $7 million and above in aviation death cases," says Mark Moller, a partner at Kreindler & Kreindler, which has been involved in suits related to the Pan Am Lockerbie disaster, the crash of an Avianca jet in New York that ran out of fuel, United flight 232's crash in Sioux City, Iowa, and others. "A settlement of $100,000 for a death case would be unusually low."

Headquarters of Major U.S. Airlines
(and Their Code-Sharing Partners);
U.S. Commuter Airlines

Airline/Phone	*Address*
Aero Coach Aviation 305-359-1591	P.O. Box 21604 Ft. Lauderdale, FL 33335
Alaska Airlines 206-433-3200	P.O. Box 68900, Seattle-Tacoma Int'l. Airport, Seattle, WA 98168-0900

ALASKA AIRLINES COMMUTER:

Bering Air 907-443-5422	P.O. Box 1650 Nome, AK 99762-1650
ERA Aviation 907-248-4422	6160 S. Airpark Drive Anchorage, AK 99502
Horizon Air Industries 206-241-6757	19521 Pacific Highway South Seattle, WA 98188
L.A.B. Flying Service 907-766-2222	P.O. Box 272 Haines, AK 99827
Temsco Airlines 907-225-9810	P.O. Box 8015 Ketchikan, AK 99901

Airline/Phone	*Address*
ALOHA AIR GROUP:	
Aloha Airlines 808-836-1111	P.O. Box 30028 Honolulu, HI 96820-0028
Aloha Islandair 808-836-7693	Commuter Terminal, Honolulu Int'l. Airport, Honolulu, HI 96819
American Airlines 817-963-1234	P.O. Box 619616, DFW Airport, TX 75261-9616
AMERICAN EAGLE:	
Chaparral Airlines 915-675-8000	P.O. Box 206 Abilene, TX 79604
Command Airways 914-462-6100	263 New Hackensack Road, Wappingers Falls, NY 12590
Executive Air Charter 809-791-8070	P.O. Box 38082, Airport Station San Juan, PR 00937-0082
Metroflight 214-453-4400	1700 West 20th St., P.O. Box 61266 DFW Airport, TX 75261
Nashville Eagle 615-399-6318	International Plaza, 2 International Drive, Suite 900, Nashville, TN 37217
Simmons Airlines 312-280-8222	900 North Franklin, Suite 800 Chicago, IL 60610
Wings West Airlines 805-541-1010	P.O. Box 8115 San Luis Obispo, CA 93403-8115
Paradise Island Airlines 305-524-0333	P.O. Box 35010, 1550 SW 43rd St. Ft. Lauderdale, FL 33304
Continental Airlines 713-834-5000	P.O. Box 4607 Houston, TX 77210-4607

Airline/Phone	Address
CONTINENTAL EXPRESS:	
Bar Harbor Airlines 713-853-9700	1301 Fannin, Suite 1425 Houston, TX 77002
Britt Airways 713-230-6600	17340 Chanute Rd. Houston, TX 77032
Rocky Mountain Airways 303-388-5354	Hangar 6, Stapleton Int'l. Airport Denver, CO 80207
Southern Jersey Airways 609-348-4600	Bader Field Airport Atlantic City, NJ 08401
Delta Air Lines 404-765-2600	Hartsfield Atlanta Int'l. Airport Atlanta, GA 30320-9998
DELTA CONNECTION:	
Atlantic Southeast Air 404-996-4562	1688 Phoenix Parkway College Park, GA 30349
Business Express 203-292-6500	Building 85-172, Bradley Int'l Airport Windsor Locks, CT 06096
Comair 606-525-2550	P.O. Box 75021 Cincinnati, OH 45275
SkyWest Airlines 801-628-2655	50 East 100 South St. George, UT 84770
Eastern Airlines 305-873-2211	Miami Int'l. Airport Miami, FL 33148-0001
EASTERN EXPRESS/EASTERN METRO EXPRESS:	
Aviation Associates 809-778-9200	P.O. Box 1686 Kingshill, St. Croix, USVI 00850

Airline/Phone	*Address*
Bar Harbor Airlines 713-853-9700	1301 Fannin, Suite 1425 Houston, TX 77002
Metro Express 404-559-9888	4854 Old National Highway, Suite 200 Atlanta, GA 30337
Hawaiian Airlines 808-525-5511	P.O. Box 30008, Honolulu Int'l. Airport Honolulu, HI 96820-0008
Midway Airlines 312-838-0001	5959 South Cicero Ave. Chicago, IL 60638-3821
MIDWAY COMMUTER:	
Midway Commuter 217-789-0095	900 Capital Airport Drive Springfield, IL 62707
Nantucket Airlines 508-228-6234	Nantucket Memorial Airport Nantucket, MA 02554
Northwest Airlines 612-726-2111	Minneapolis-St. Paul Int'l. Airport St. Paul, MN 55111-3075
NORTHWEST AIRLINK:	
Big Sky Transportation 406-245-9449	P.O. Box 31397 Billings, MT 59107
Express Airlines I 404-991-3300	1777 Phoenix Parkway, Suite 303 Atlanta, GA 30349
Horizon Air Industries 206-241-6757	19521 Pacific Highway South Seattle, WA 98188
Mesaba Airlines 612-726-5151	7501 NW 26th Ave. South Minneapolis, MN 55450
Northeast Express **Regional Airlines** 207-942-9303	136 Union Street Bangor, ME 04401

Airline/Phone	Address
Precision Valley Aviation 603-668-0082	841 Galaxy Way Manchester, NH 03103
Pan American 212-880-1234	Pan Am Building New York, NY 10166-0001

PAN AM EXPRESS/PAN AM COMMUTER:

Pan Am Express 215-961-2200	NE Philadelphia Airport, Grant Ave. & Ashton Rd. Philadelphia, PA 19114
Scenic Airlines 702-739-5611	241 East Reno Ave. Las Vegas, NV 89119
Southwest Airlines 214-902-1101	Box 37611 Love Field Dallas, TX 75235-1625
StatesWest Airlines 602-220-0391	4909 East McDowell Road, Suite 105 Phoenix, AZ 85008-4227
Trans World Airlines 212-242-3000	100 South Bedford Rd. Mt. Kisco, NY 10549

TRANS WORLD EXPRESS

Air Midwest 316-942-8137	P.O. Box 7724 Wichita, KS 67277
Jet Express 609-345-2230	Bader Field Airport Atlantic City, NJ 08401
Metro Airlines NE 518-561-5305	Clinton County Airport Plattsburgh, NY 12901
Trans States Airlines 314-739-7300	3990 Fee Fee Rd. St. Louis, MO 63044
United Airlines 312-952-4000	P.O. Box 66100 Chicago, IL 60666-0100

Airline/Phone	Address
UNITED EXPRESS:	
Air Wisconsin 414-739-5123	203 Challenger Drive Appleton, WI 54915
Aspen Airways 303-320-4747	3980 Quebec St. Denver, CO 80207
Atlantic Coast Airways 703-209-0096	111-M Carpenter Drive, Suite #8 Sterling, VA 22170
Mesa Airlines 505-327-0271	1296 West Navajo Street Farmington, NM 87401
NPA 509-545-6420	1135 East Hillsboro Pasco, WA 99301
WestAir Commuter Airlines 209-294-6915	5570 Air Terminal Drive Fresno, CA 93727
USAir 703-418-7000	2345 Crystal Drive, Crystal Park 4 Arlington, VA 22227
USAIR EXPRESS:	
CCAir 704-527-7670	9401 Arrowpoint Blvd., Suite 300 Charlotte, NC 28217
Chautauqua Airlines 716-664-2400	RD 1, Chautauqua County Airport Jamestown, NY 14701
Commutair 518-562-2700	Clinton County Airport Plattsburgh, NY 12901
Crown Airways 814-371-2691	DuBois-Jefferson County Airport PO Box 377 Falls Creek, PA 15840
Henson Aviation 301-742-2996	Salisbury/Wicomico County Airport Salisbury, MD 21801
Jetstream Int'l Airlines 513-454-1116	6520 Poe Ave., Suite 400 Dayton, OH 45414

Airline/Phone	*Address*
Pennsylvania Commuter Airlines 717-944-2781	Harrisburg Int'l. Airport Middletown, PA 17057
Allegheny Commuter Airlines 215-375-8551	P.O. Box 1201 Reading, PA 19603
Vieques Air Link 809-741-3261	P.O. Box 487 Vieques, PR 00765

Source: Air Transport Association; Regional Airline Association.

APPENDIX B

State Consumer Protection Offices/Attorneys General/Ombudsmen

State/Phone	Address
Alabama 800-392-5658 205-261-7334	Director, Consumer Protection Division, Office of Attorney General 11 South Union St. Montgomery, AL 36130
Alaska 907-279-0428	Chief, Consumer Protection Section, Office of Attorney General 1031 West Fourth Ave., Suite 110-B Anchorage, AK 99501
Arizona 800-352-8431 602-542-3702	Chief Counsel, Financial Fraud Division, Office of Attorney General 1275 West Washington St. Phoenix, AZ 85007
Arkansas 800-482-8982 501-682-2007	Director, Consumer Protection Division, Office of Attorney General 200 Tower Building, 4th and Center Streets Little Rock, AR 72201
California 916-445-0660	Director, California Department of Consumer Affairs 1020 N St. Sacramento, CA 95814
800-952-5225 800-952-5548 916-322-3360	Public Inquiry Unit, Office of Attorney General 1515 K St., Suite 511, P.O. Box 944255 Sacramento, CA 94244

State/Phone	Address
Colorado 303-866-5167	Chief, Consumer Protection Unit Office of Attorney General 1525 Sherman St. 3rd floor Denver, CO 80203
Connecticut 800-842-2649 203-566-4999	Commissioner, Department of Consumer Protection State Office Building 165 Capitol Ave. Hartford, CT 06106
203-566-5374	Assistant Attorney General, Antitrust/Consumer Protection, Office of Attorney General 100 Sherman St. Hartford, CT 06105
Delaware 302-571-3250	Director, Division of Consumer Affairs Department of Community Affairs 820 North French St., 4th floor Wilmington, DE 19801
302-571-3849	Deputy-in-Charge, Economic Crime/Consumer Rights Division, Office of Attorney General 820 North French St. Wilmington, DE 19801
District of Columbia 202-727-7000	Director, Department of Consumer and Regulatory Affairs 614 H St., NW Washington, DC 20001
Florida 800-327-3382 904-488-2226	Director, Department of Agriculture & Consumer Services, Division of Consumer Services 218 Mayo Building Tallahassee, FL 32399
305-377-5619	Chief, Consumer Litigation Section, Consumer Protection Division, Office of Attorney General 401 NW Second Ave., Suite 921N Miami, FL 33128

State/Phone	Address
Georgia 800-282-5808 404-656-7000	Administrator, Governor's Office of Consumer Affairs 2 Martin Luther King Jr., Drive. SE Plaza Level—East Tower Atlanta GA 30334
Hawaii 808-548-2540	Director, Office of Consumer Protection Department of Commerce and Consumer Affairs 828 Fort Street Mall, P.O. Box 3767 Honolulu, HI 96812
Illinois 800-642-3112 217-782-0244	Director, Governor's Office of Citizen's Assistance 201 West Monroe St. Springfield, IL 62706
312-917-3580	Chief, Consumer Protection Division, Office of Attorney General 100 West Randolph, 12th floor Chicago, IL 60601
Indiana 800-382-5516 317-232-6330	Chief Counsel and Director, Consumer Protection Division, Office of Attorney General 219 State House Indianapolis, IN 46204
Iowa 800-358-5510 515-281-3592	Iowa Citizens' Aide/Ombudsman 215 East 7th St., Capitol Complex Des Moines, IA 50319
515-281-5926	Assistant Attorney General, Consumer Protection Division, Office of Attorney General 1300 East Walnut St., 2nd floor Des Moines, IA 50319
Kansas 800-432-2310 913-296-3751	Deputy Attorney General, Consumer Protection Division, Office of Attorney General Kansas Judicial Center Topeka, KS 66612

State/Phone	Address
Kentucky 800-432-9257 502-564-2200	Director, Consumer Protection Division, Office of Attorney General 209 Saint Clair St. Frankfort, KY 40601
Louisiana 504-342-7013	Chief, Consumer Protection Section, Office of Attorney General State Capitol Building, P.O. Box 94005 Baton Rouge, LA 70804
Maine 207-289-3716	Chief, Consumer and Antitrust Division Office of Attorney General State House Station #6 Augusta, ME 04333
Maryland 800-492-2114 301-528-8662	Chief, Consumer Protection Division, Office of Attorney General Seven North Calvert St. Baltimore, MD 21202
Massachusetts 617-727-8400	Chief, Consumer Protection Division, Department of Attorney General 131 Tremont Place Boston, MA 02111
617-727-7780	Secretary, Executive Office of Consumer Affairs and Business Regulation One Ashburton Place, Room 1411 Boston, MA 02108
Michigan 517-373-1140	Assistant Attorney General, Consumer Protection Division, Office of Attorney General 670 Law Building Lansing, MI 48913
517-373-0947	Executive Director, Michigan Consumers Council 414 Hollister Building 106 West Allegan St. Lansing, MI 48933

State/Phone	Address
Minnesota 612-296-2331	Director of Consumer Services, Office of Attorney General 117 University Ave. St. Paul, MN 55155
Mississippi 601-354-6018	Special Assistant Attorney General and Chief, Consumer Protection Division Office of Attorney General, P.O. Box 220 Jackson MS 39205
Missouri 800-392-8222 314-751-2616	Chief Counsel, Trade Offense Division Office of Attorney General, P.O. Box 899 Jefferson City, MO 65102
Montana 406-444-4312	Consumer Affairs Unit, Department of Commerce 1424 Ninth Ave. Helena, MT 59620
Nebraska 402-471-4723	Assistant Attorney General, Consumer Protection Division Department of Justice 2115 State Capitol, P.O. Box 98920 Lincoln, NE 68509
Nevada 702-486-4150	Commissioner of Consumer Affairs, Department of Commerce State Mail Room Complex Las Vegas, NV 89158
New Hampshire 603-271-3641	Chief, Consumer Protection and Antitrust Division Office of Attorney General, State House Annex Concord, NH 03301
New Jersey 201-648-4010	Director, Division of Consumer Affairs 1100 Raymond Blvd., Room 504 Newark, NJ 07102
800-792-8600 609-292-7087	Commissioner, Department of the Public Advocate CN 850, Justice Complex Trenton, NJ 08625

State/Phone	Address
201-648-4730	Assistant Attorney General, Division of Law, Office of Attorney General 1100 Raymond Blvd., Room 316 Newark, NJ 07102
New Mexico 800-432-2070 505-872-6910	Director, Consumer and Economic Crime Division Office of Attorney General, P.O. Drawer 1508 Santa Fe, NM 87504
New York 518-474-8583	Chairperson and Executive Director, New York State Consumer Protection Board 99 Washington Ave. Albany, NY 12210
518-474-5481	Assistant Attorney General, Bureau of Consumer Frauds and Protection Office of Attorney General, State Capitol Albany, NY 12224
North Carolina 919-733-7741	Special Deputy Attorney General, Consumer Protection Section Office of Attorney General Department of Justice Building, P.O. Box 629 Raleigh, NC 27602
North Dakota 800-472-2600 701-224-3404	Director, Consumer Fraud Division Office of Attorney General, 600 East Boulevard Bismarck, ND 58505
Ohio 800-282-0515 614-466-4986	Chief, Consumer Frauds and Crimes Section, Office of Attorney General State Office Tower, 25th floor 30 East Broad St. Columbus, OH 43266
800-282-9448 614-466-9605	Consumers' Counsel 77 South High Street, 15th Floor Columbus, OH 43266

State/Phone	Address
Oklahoma 405-521-3921	Assistant Attorney General for Consumer Affairs, Office of Attorney General 112 State Capitol Building Oklahoma City, OK 73105
Oregon 503-378-4320	Attorney in Charge, Financial Fraud Section Department of Justice, Justice Building Salem, OR 97310
Pennsylvania 800-441-2555 717-787-9707	Director, Bureau of Consumer Protection, Office of Attorney General Strawberry Square, 14th floor Harrisburg, PA 17120
Rhode Island 401-277-2104	Director, Consumer Protection Division, Department of Attorney General 72 Pine St. Providence, RI 02903
401-277-2764	Executive Director, Rhode Island Consumers' Council 365 Broadway Providence, RI 02909
South Carolina 803-734-3970	Assistant Attorney General, Consumer Fraud and Antitrust Section, Office of Attorney General P.O. Box 11549 Columbia, SC 29211
800-922-1594 803-734-9452	Administrator, Department of Consumer Affairs P.O. Box 5757 Columbia, SC 29250
803-734-0457	State Ombudsman, Office of Executive Policy and Program 1205 Pendleton St., Room 308 Columbia, SC 29201
South Dakota 605-773-4400	Assistant Attorney General, Division of Consumer Affairs, Office of Attorney General State Capitol Building Pierre, SD 57501

State/Phone	Address
Tennessee 615-741-2672	Deputy Attorney General, Antitrust and Consumer Protection Division, Office of Attorney General 450 James Robertson Parkway Nashville, TN 37219
800-342-8385 615-741-4737	Director, Division of Consumer Affairs Department of Commerce and Insurance 500 James Robertson Parkway, 5th Floor Nashville, TN 37219
Texas 512-463-2070	Assistant Attorney General and Chief, Consumer Protection Division, Office of Attorney General Capitol Station, P.O. Box 12548 Austin, TX 78711
Utah 801-530-6601	Director, Division of Consumer Protection Department of Commerce 160 East 3rd South, P.O. Box 45802 Salt Lake City, UT 84145
801-538-1331	Assistant Attorney General for Consumer Affairs, Office of Attorney General 115 State Capitol Salt Lake City, UT 84114
Vermont 802-828-3171	Assistant Attorney General and Chief, Public Protection Division, Office of Attorney General 109 State St. Montpelier, VT 05602
Virginia 800-451-1525 804-786-2116	Senior Assistant Attorney General, Antitrust and Consumer Litigation Section, Office of Attorney General Supreme Court Building 101 North Eighth St. Richmond, VA 23219

State/Phone	Address
800-552-9963 804-786-2042	Director, Office of Consumer Affairs, Department of Agriculture and Consumer Services Room 101, Washington Building 1100 Bank St. Richmond, VA 23219
Washington 206-753-6210	Investigator, Consumer and Business, Fair Practices Division, Office of Attorney General North 122 Capitol Way Olympia, WA 98501
West Virginia 800-368-8808 304-348-8986	Director, Consumer Protection Division, Office of Attorney General 812 Quarrier St., 6th floor Charleston, WV 25301
Wisconsin 800-362-3020 608-266-9836	Administrator, Division of Trade and Consumer Protection Department of Agriculture Trade and Consumer Protection 801 West Badger Rd., P.O. Box 8911 Madison, WI 53708
800-362-8189 608-266-1852	Assistant Attorney General, Office of Consumer Protection Department of Justice, P.O. Box 7856 Madison, WI 53707
Wyoming 307-777-6286	Assistant Attorney General, Office of Attorney General 123 State Capitol Building Cheyenne, WY 82002

Source: U.S. Office of Consumer Affairs.

APPENDIX C

Better Business Bureau (BBB) Offices in Major Airline Headquarters Locations

Airline	Headquarters City	BBB Phone Number
Alaska Airlines	Seattle, WA	206-448-8888
Aloha Airlines	Honolulu, HI	808-942-2355
American Airlines	Dallas, TX	214-220-2000
Braniff	Orlando, FL	402-660-9500
Continental	Houston, TX	713-868-9500
Delta Air Lines	Atlanta, GA	404-688-4910
Eastern Airlines	Miami, FL	305-625-1302
Hawaiian Airlines	Honolulu, HI	808-942-2355
Midway Airlines	Chicago, IL	312-346-3313
Northwest Airlines	St. Paul, MN	612-699-1111
Pan Am	New York, NY	212-533-6200
Southwest Airlines	Dallas, TX	214-220-2000
TWA	Mt. Kisco, NY	914-428-1230
United Airlines	Chicago, IL	312-346-3313
USAir	Arlington, VA	703-276-0100

Source: Council of Better Business Bureaus.

APPENDIX D

Government/Consumer/Professional Overseers

Agency or Association/Phone	Address
American Society of Travel Agents 703-739-2782	Director, Consumer Affairs P.O. Box 23992 Washington, DC 20026
International Airline Passengers Association 800-527-5888 214-404-9980	Consumer Affairs Department P.O. Box 870188 Dallas, TX 75287
U.S. Tour Operators Association 212-944-5727	President 211 East 51st St., Suite 12-B New York, NY 10022
U.S. Dept. of Commerce 202-377-5001	Office of Consumer Affairs, Room 5718 Washington, DC 20230
Aviation Consumer Action Project (ACAP)	P.O. Box 19029 Washington, DC 20036
U.S. Department of Transportation 202-366-2220	Consumer Affairs Division, Room 10405 Office of Community and Consumer Affairs, USDOT 400 7th Street, SW Washington, DC 20590
Federal Aviation Administration 800-424-9393 202-366-0123	Community and Consumer Liaison Division FAA (APA-200), USDOT Washington, DC 20591

APPENDIX E

National Media Outlets Reporting on Consumer Air Topics

Publication	Address
Ready for Take-off	P.O. Box 521 Easton, PA 18044-0521
Consumers Digest Magazine	5705 North Lincoln Ave. Chicago, IL 60659
Consumer Reports Magazine	256 Washington St. Mount Vernon, NY 10553
Money Magazine	TimeLife Building Rockefeller Center New York, NY 10020

Selected List of Attorneys Specializing in Aviation Litigation

Attorney	Law Firm/Phone	Address
John Breit	Breit, Best, Richman & Bosch 303-573-7777	1512 Larimer Suite 900 Denver, CO 80202
John J. Kennelly	John J. Kennelly & Associates 312-346-3546	111 West Washington St. Suite 1449 Chicago, IL 60602
Francis Flemming Lee Kreindler Mark Moller	Kreindler & Kreindler 212-687-8181	100 Park Ave. 18th floor New York, NY 10017
Wm. Marshal Morgan	Morgan, Wenzel, McNicholas 213-483-1961	1545 Wilshire Boulevard Suite 800 Los Angeles, CA 90017
Aaron Podhurst	Podhurst, Orseck, Josefsberg, Eaton, Mendow, Olin, & Perwin 305-358-2800	25 West Flagler St. Suite 800 Miami, FL 33130
Richard Schaden	Schaden, Lampert, & Lampert 303-786-8074	1655 Walnut Street Boulder, CO 80302

Source: Aviation attorney recommendations.

About the Authors

Marie Hodge and Jeff Blyskal are an award-winning investigative reporting team who have written extensively on consumer, business, personal finance, and education topics for a variety of leading publications.

In 1984, Hodge and Blyskal won a National Magazine Award for their groundbreaking *New York* magazine investigative cover story that examined and rated New York banks. They have appeared on numerous broadcasts in connection with their work, including "Good Morning America," "CBS News Nightwatch," CNN, "McLaughlin," and the ABC radio network.